★ The London housewife, with little musical training, who creates hundreds of compositions dictated to her by the spirits of famous dead composers.

★ Children who have vivid memories of their former lives.

★ The amazing case of Grace Rosher who receives ghost-written messages from her dead fiancé.

★ The evangelist faith-healer who fills cavities by prayer.

MARVELS AND WONDERS THAT READ LIKE FANTASY BUT ARE SCIENTIFICALLY DOCUMENTED!

Other SIGNET Books You'll Want to Read

Probing the
UNEXPLAINED

by
Allen Spraggett

A SIGNET BOOK
NEW AMERICAN LIBRARY
TIMES MIRROR

For my mother and father . . .
wherever you are.

I am grateful to all the researchers, and all the unusually gifted people, whose work made this book possible; especially for their kindness in giving to me so freely of their time and themselves.

Also, I am grateful to my editor, Katharine Kidde, for seeing me through another difficult delivery. . . .

CONTENTS

PART I

At the Edge of the Unexplained: Unsolved Mysteries

ONE

Atlantis: Cayce's Lost Continent Found?

Off Bimini, in clear azure waters, a symbol of man's deepest hopes and fears may be emerging from mystery and mud into the realm of reality. . . .

EDGAR CAYCE, the famed Sleeping Prophet, made at least two specific predictions about the re-emergence of the legendary lost continent of Atlantis.

The first, uttered during one of his strange sleeplike trances on December 20, 1933, included a reference to "the sunken portion of Atlantis, or Poseidia, where a portion of the temple may yet be discovered under the slime of ages of sea water—near what is known as Bimini, off the coast of Florida."

The second prediction, made by Cayce on June 28, 1940, declared: "Poseidia will be among the first portions of Atlantis to rise again. Expect it in '68 and '69. Not so far away."

In the spring of 1968 a Florida cargo pilot named Robert Brush sighted what looked like a sunken building a few miles off the island of Andros, a neighbor of Bimini, in the Bahamas. That was the first glimpse of what, according to investigating scientists, may be a remnant of myth-shrouded Atlantis.

If this proves to be true it will be the most significant archeological find of our time, possibly of all time. It may mean the rewriting of history.

The find, originally thought to consist of the ruins of two buildings about six feet below the ocean's surface, now encompasses the remains of what appears to have been a vast city. There are huge, elaborate edifices. Also, a paved road, perfectly preserved, runs for miles underwater.

On-the-spot investigations were led by Dr. Manson Valentine, honorary curator of the Science Museum of

Miami and research associate of Honolulu's Bishop Museum, and Dr. Dmitri Rebikoff, French-born oceanographer and marine explorer noted for his invention of the Pegasus underwater diver propulsion unit.

In the early stages of their investigation, before the full extent of the find was realized, Valentine and Rebikoff were quoted as speculating on whether the site was linked to Atlantis. Valentine, a student of Edgar Cayce's thought, declared himself a firm believer in the historicity of the lost continent, a point of doctrine which is not accepted by the typical scientist. Rebikoff, from the quotations attributed to him, was more cautious but definitely open-minded on the subject.

"I believe there was an Atlantis," Valentine said flatly in a report in the *Miami Herald* of September 12, 1968, "and not because of mythical references to it but because of facts. These consist of various pieces of evidence that I've personally found in explorations in Yucatan, South America, Mexico, and the West Indies."

Of the Bahamian site, Valentine remarked: "Whether we have here an Atlantean or post-cataclysmic artifact of upwards of ten thousand years is too early to conjecture upon. But what seems certain is that the ruin is pre-Columbian, as established by its position relative to the present water level."

In the same press story Rebikoff was quoted: "Atlantis is generally considered a myth but frequently archeology has a way of proving out a myth." He added, "I'm not a follower of these psychics who claim knowledge of Atlantis but in this particular case they might turn out to be accurate."

The oceanographer theorized that Atlantis "existed as a very large body of land that occupied most of the Atlantic and was broken up by cataclysm.

"Its people must have been technologically advanced, although I definitely don't believe some of the psychic theories that the inhabitants had airplanes and cars. This is utterly ridiculous and just doesn't bear inspection.

"But there is an artifact that would indicate some type of technological sophistication on their part. In Glastonbury, England, there is a thirty-mile-wide ring of raised ground called the Great Zodiac. It's visible only from the air and includes representations of the twelve zodiacal figures. Carbon-dating tests have shown this formation to be between ten and twenty thousand years old."

3

Rebikoff noted that the find in the Bahamas also resembled structures in sunken cities he had explored in the Mediterranean Sea.

What does tradition, and Edgar Cayce's psychic lore, tell us about Atlantis?

The earliest known reference to the subject is in two dialogues of Plato dating from the fifth century B.C. In one, Plato introduces Atlantis in a discussion between Solon, one of the earliest Greek sages, and certain Egyptian priests who place the disappearance of the continent nine thousand years earlier.

Plato said the fabled land sank into the ocean after a stupendous natural convulsion. He described the destruction as follows: "There occurred portentous earthquakes and floods, and one grievous day and night befell them when . . . the island of Atlantis . . . was swallowed up by the sea and vanished."

Plato said the sunken continent had been the home of a glittering civilization versed in the arts and sciences.

Edgar Cayce, in his readings, described Atlantis in a way which, even to some of his greatest admirers, strains credulity. He linked the demise of that glamorous civilization to the misuse of a technology more dazzling than ours.

According to Cayce, talking in his strange sleep, there were three periods of destruction in the history of Atlantis. The first two were about 15,600 B.C. when the Atlantean land mass broke up into five giant islands, the three largest being Poseidia, Aryan, and Og. The third phase of destruction came about 10,000 B.C. when the three main islands were swallowed up overnight, along with portions of the other two.

There were waves of refugees, said Cayce, who spread out into Egypt, parts of Europe, and Central and South America, seeding advanced civilizations in these areas.

Before the final dissolution, he declared, the Atlanteans became increasingly inhumane in the application of their advanced technology, which included some sort of giant laser device used both as an energy source to power their cities and as a death ray. Cayce suggested that the ultimate catastrophe resulted partly from something analogous to an uncontrolled nuclear reaction.

Dr. Rebikoff's skepticism notwithstanding, Cayce pictured Atlantis as a place where the inhabitants had flying

4

craft, submarine vessels, and vehicles similar to automobiles.

Such things, as I've allowed, take some believing, even for Cayce's devoted followers. But, to be sure, there are some modern discoveries which lend a certain credibility to the picture of an ancient Atlantean civilization complete with radio, television, and a power source comparable to nuclear energy.

Recently a group of reputable scientists who call themselves the Society for the Investigation of the Unexplained, whose president is the noted zoologist-author, Ivan Sanderson, raised the question of whether there were ancient cultures which used electricity. The question was provoked by a curious wall painting in a temple at Dendera, Egypt.

This "puzzling and provocative picture suggests a possible residue of a higher technology which subsequent civilizations lost," said the *Journal of the Society for the Investigation of the Unexplained*.

The picture depicts what presumably is a religious ritual (since it is in a temple). Two huge priestlike figures are carrying a pair of objects which look astonishingly like enormous light bulbs containing heavy filaments. The objects are resting on pedestals which closely resemble modern insulation fixtures for very high-tension power lines.

An electrical engineer who studied the picture said that slight variations between the two fixtures to which the "light bulbs" are attached suggest that they could be positive and negative electrical terminals.

Parallels to this picture have turned up in paintings found on ceramics in South America, according to the *Journal of the Society for the Investigation of the Unexplained*. "These paintings," said the journal, "appear on detailed analysis by competent experts to be formalized layouts for electronic circuitry."

Actually, as long as thirty or more years ago discoveries were made which also pointed to a knowledge of electricity by some cultures of antiquity.

In 1936 Dr. William Koenig of the Iraq Museum found an ancient battery among relics of the Parthian kingdom, which existed from 250 B.C. to A.D. 224. The object was a clay vase containing a cylinder made of sheet copper, the inner surface of which was covered with a thin layer of asphalt. A thick plug of asphalt was forced into the upper end of the cylinder. In the center of the plug was a solid piece of iron.

Such a device was demonstrably capable of generating an electric current and this appears to have been its only conceivable purpose. But to what use was it put?

Well, when the find was made, more than three decades ago, silversmiths in Iraq and other Middle East countries were using a crude method of electrogilding their wares, that is, gold-plating them. Since a galvanic battery of the type found would produce current strong enough to electrogild small articles it is plausible that this was one use for it. There may well have been others.

Similar ancient batteries have been found by other archeologists. Professor Erik Kuehnel of Berlin dug up several dating from the dynasty of the Sassanids who ruled Persia from A.D. 224 to A. D. 651.

There is even earlier evidence, dating from 2000 B.C., of electroplating of metal among the Egyptians. Copper and bronze vessels and other art objects taken from Egyptian tombs have been found to be plated with antimony, a silverlike metal. The exact method of metal plating used probably was a trade secret of the Egyptian priests, who were in many ways the great-grandfathers of today's scientists.

If priests used electricity to plate art objects four thousand years ago in Egypt, did this knowledge represent the glimmerings of an embryo science or the residue of a higher technology from the still more distant past?

A Soviet astrophysicist, N. K. Agrest, thinks the earth shows traces of ancient nuclear experiments. He speculates that tektites, mysterious glasslike stones that are found in various parts of the world and contain radioactive isotopes of aluminum and beryllium, are the remains of these tests.

The idea that ancient man may have known the secret of flight is suggested by an amazing set of documents called the Piri Reis maps. These once belonged to a nineteenth-century Turkish naval officer, Admiral Piri Reis.

What has astounded modern cartographers—such as Arlington H. Mallery and Father Daniel Lineham of Boston's Weston Observatory—is that these maps reproduce the geography and even topography of many regions of the earth with an accuracy that implies they were based on an aerial survey.

Mallery, a prominent American cartographer, said in

1952 that the Piri Reis maps depicted not only the Mediterranean and Middle East but North and South America, and even the contours of an unglaciated Antarctic. Certain mountain ranges in Antarctica which were not discovered until 1952 appear on the maps.

Professor Charles Hapgood of the University of New Hampshire has suggested that a comparison of the Piri Reis maps with photographs of the earth taken from space satellites indicates that the originals may have been aerial photographs taken from an enormous altitude.

By space visitors or by flying Atlantean map-makers?

In April, 1969, I met Manson Valentine and discussed with him the archeological find in the Bahamas. He showed me photographs of the site, taken both underwater and from the air, and let me examine chunks of stone from the submerged structures.

At that time, the site included the remains of six buildings. (Later, as we shall see, it proved to be much more extensive.) Each building was about one hundred feet long and sixty feet wide, or roughly the size of a modern suburban house lot.

The central building, which the investigating scientists thought was a temple, had stone walls three feet thick and an ornate style of architecture. On the archeological premise that where you find a templelike structure you generally find a city around it, Valentine said he hoped to uncover many more buildings buried in the ocean mud and slime.

The six structures were clearly visible in aerial photographs Valentine showed me, taken from an altitude of five hundred feet. They appeared as huge dark rectangles in the clear ocean.

The undersea road, which ran from the land into the water, was paved with stone slabs, Valentine said, each 2½ feet long by 1½ feet wide by 8 inches thick. He told me he had traced this road for several miles to the edge of a drop-off near Andros where the ocean floor suddenly plunged one hundred fifty feet.

Valentine photographed stone monoliths as big as automobiles, man-made in his judgment, which extended in parallel rows for miles under the ocean. Also, aerial photographs depicted enormous circular shapes clearly visible in much deeper water, which Valentine believed to be structures.

"At the end of Abaco Island, near Andros, there is a

7

perfectly rectangular basin partly underwater," the scientist said. "It, like many similar structures, can be seen only from the air. It has a small channel that evidently led fresh water into it. Now it's covered with brush and no one seems to know anything about it. If it dated from Colonial times, for example, I'm sure someone in the area would have some idea of its origin."

Valentine—whose academic background includes a Ph.D. in zoology from Yale, several university teaching posts (at Yale, the University of North Carolina, and elsewhere), and a term as curator of the Alabama Museum of Natural History—has spent years studying the remains of early civilizations in Central and South America and the Pacific. He said the submerged ruins indicated that the area from Florida to the Bahamas which is now ocean was once a solid land mass. The underwater remains, he emphasized, were in his judgment definitely pre-Columbian and probably ten to twelve thousand years old.

Valentine said that he believed Atlantis was technologically advanced far beyond any other ancient civilization, maybe as advanced as Cayce claimed, and that it was wiped out virtually without a trace some one hundred twenty centuries ago.

The dissolution probably occurred in stages, he said, by a succession of cataclysms, each more devastating than the last; before the continent's final death throes there were waves of migration to what is now Europe, the Middle East, and Central and South America. Thus, the culture of parts of Europe, Egypt, and of such peoples in America as the Mayas and the Incas, may have had a common Atlantean origin.

The Atlanteans were predominantly light-skinned, Valentine suggested, and in the Americas they intermarried with the dark-skinned Indians who probably came later.

"There are intriguing bits of evidence to support this theory," Valentine said. "Pizarro found blond and red-headed Incas and the lighter their color the higher up the social hierarchy they were.

"The gods of ancient Mexico were bearded and white, like Quetzalcoatl, the white god of the Aztecs who was reputed to have taught them their arts and sciences.

"There are linguistic clues. Artifacts have been found on an island in the mouth of the Amazon bearing inscriptions in a language which is Cretan or Greek in nature. In northern Brazil there is a tribe today whose

8

language shows remnants of Etruscan. And there are other South American tribes that speak a tongue similar to Basque."

Interestingly, Edgar Cayce declared in several readings that the Basques of northern Spain, and their idiosyncratic language, were purely Atlantean.

Manson Valentine argued that if concrete evidence of the existence of Atlantis were found it would profoundly change the standard view of history.

"One thing it would mean, at the very least, is that history has proceeded not by gradual evolution but by cataclysmic evolution—tremendous natural upheavals that literally changed the face of the globe in the twinkling of an eye."

Not everybody who looked at the site off Bimini and Andros was persuaded that it represented a link with fabled Atlantis. As a matter of fact, some investigators suggested that the underwater structures near Andros were merely turtle or sponge pens built recently by local Bahamians, or, at the earliest, by the Lucayan Indians who inhabited the area when Columbus arrived. Manson Valentine rejected this theory.

"The structures may indeed have been used as turtle crawls by the local people," he told me, "but the structures themselves are undoubtedly symbolic in design. Some, for instance, are hexagonal and one is shaped like an immense sword."

The Lucayan Indians of Columbus' time did not work with stone, so far as is known, he added.

Valentine was supported in this judgment by Robert F. Marx, contributing editor on marine archeology to *Argosy*. In the December, 1969, issue of that magazine, Marx described his own on-the-spot investigation of the Bahamain site.

"Having seen and investigated this structure [the building close to Andros which was the first sighted] I find assertions that it was probably a pen used by modern Bahamians for storing turtles, sponges or conch shells baseless," Marx said.

"For the simple fact is that no one would have gone to so much trouble to make such a pen of stone blocks when they always make these pens a great deal smaller and out of wood. Furthermore the depth of water on this site is only three to four feet and this is much too shallow for the

9

boats generally used by fishermen to approach such a pen to deposit anything."

Marx confirmed in his article that the submerged ruins were huge, appeared definitely to be man-made, and, so far as he was concerned, "it is not too far out to believe that it [one of the structures] might belong to Atlantis."

Marx cited some of the reasons why the theory of a widespread civilization in the region of the Americas which was suddenly submerged seemed increasingly credible.

He noted that in 1966 a reaearch vessel doing oceanographic explorations off the coast of Peru recorded with its underwater cameras what is believed to be the site of an ancient civilization. On a muddy plain six thousand feet beneath the ocean stood ornately carved columns bearing writing of some sort. Nearby, sonar devices detected strange "lumps" on the ocean bed, probably ruins of buildings.

In 1959 the U. S. Coast and Geodetic Survey reported that, during hydrographic studies off the Florida Keys, sinkholes as big as a half-mile in diameter were discovered in depths of nine hundred feet. These, located some fourteen miles from shore, are presumed to have been freshwater lakes in an area which in now under the sea.

In 1898, a ship laying a submarine cable near the Azores (which Cayce said were the peaks of one portion of submerged Atlantis), in water two miles deep, brought up specimens of lava of a vitreous nature—meaning it must have solidified in the open air because lava which hardens under water assumes a different, crystalline structure. Since lava decomposes at a certain rate under water, scientists calculated that this area of the ocean's floor had been dry land no more than fifteen thousand years ago.

In mid-1971 I received a progress report on the Bahamian site from Manson Valentine. He said very recent discoveries had strengthened his opinion that the find probably was Atlantean.

Near Bimini, he reported, there were "megalithic" remains of what appeared to be "a vast metropolitan complex covering thousands and thousands of acres." Huge sculptured columns and what may be the tip of a giant pyramid protruding from the ocean silt have been found at a depth of twenty feet.

How old are the ruins?

"We consulted one of the world's leading marine archeologists," Valentine said. "Using carbon-dating he estimated that fossil mangrove material associated with the ruins at the twelve-foot level are six thousand years old. Those at twenty feet are much older, indicating the structures at that depth probably are twelve thousand years old.

"This would make it the oldest archeological site in the world."

The expert had examined the style of the undersea architecture, said Valentine, and pronounced it "Cyclopean," the style used by the earliest civilizations, not only in Europe and Asia but also in America.

No one knows how extensive the site really is, Manson Valentine noted. The ruins appear to extend at least eighty miles, the approximate distance between Andros and Bimini, but they go even beyond that. One "enormous structure" in very deep water is so huge, he said, that it is perfectly visible from the air at an altitude of thirty thousand feet.

Valentine contended that whatever it was that caused the submersion of such an extended area "must have been a cataclysmic thing." He speculated that it was related to the reversal of the earth's magnetic poles, an eventuality —actually, a sort of planetary short-circuit—which would cause the earth to stop spinning on its axis and then reverse its direction of rotation.

Under such unimaginable stress the earth's crust would crumble, the ocean floor heave, mountains rise, and whole continents would be engulfed by boiling seas. The phenomenon of polar reversal is seriously proposed by Immanuel Velikovsky in his controversial books, *Worlds in Collision* and *Ages in Chaos,* as an explanation for certain geological anomalies.

Meanwhile, investigations continue on the mysterious site near Bimini. Whether it proves to be indeed a portion of Atlantis, or the remnants of another very early American civilization, is too soon to tell. Nevertheless, Edgar Cayce's words, uttered forty years ago, seem eerily apposite: " . . . a portion of the temple may yet be discovered under the slime of ages of sea water—near what is known as Bimini. . . ."

11

TWO

The Rehabiliation
of Astrology

*From Atlantis to the stars isn't all that
far. Astrology, the ancient scientific art
once more coming into its own, may
provide a link not only between man and
his universe but between man and his
past. . . .*

SYDNEY OMARR is sought after by the rich and
famous.

Movie stars—such as Mae West, Jennifer Jones, and
the late Jayne Mansfield—have been known to make pil-
grimages to his Hollywood Hills home seeking counsel for
their private and professional lives. Writers, philosophers,
and politicians—such as Henry Miller (*Tropic of Cancer*), Aldous Huxley, and former California governor
Goodwin Knight—have extolled his wisdom and benefited
from his services.

Sydney Omarr is not a doctor, psychoanalyst, or tax
consultant. He's an astrologer.

For a fee, he prepares a client's horoscope—a chart of
the sky as it was at the moment of the person's birth, showing the relative position of all the planets in the solar
system—and on the basis of such a chart offers advice
on matters of love, money, and health ("the three reasons
why most people come," says Omarr, "in that order").

He may be the most successful practitioner of the "scientific art" of astrology (he compares it to medicine in the
sense of being both an art and a science) since Kepler and
Newton, both great astronomers who were also astrologers.
Time magazine called this former newsman—Omarr
used to be head of CBS radio news in Los Angeles—
"astrology's most articulate protagonist."

Syndicated in nearly three hundred newspapers, with
his daily column currently being read in seventeen lan-
guages, the author of several successful books, and a

frequent guest on national radio and television shows, Omarr symbolizes what is for some observers one of the most curious paradoxes of our time—the rebirth of the ancient "superstition" of astrology when science had declared it to be dead beyond recall.

Astrology is currently enjoying a vogue it has not had for many, many years. Millions consult their horoscopes in the daily newspapers as religiously as they used to say their prayers (and complain like mad to the editor if the horoscope doesn't appear), astrology books are doing a booming business, and jewelry and even clothes with astrological motifs are "in."

Sydney Omarr is both a symptom and a cause of the phenomenon.

He doesn't look like a throwback to the Middle Ages, garbed in conical cap and robe embroidered with crescent moons. He is in in his forties, personable, dresses like a bank president or a corporation lawyer, and on the subject of astrology is ready to talk and talk and talk. And he talks well, as I found out when I first interviewed him in Hollywood and as I've continued to find out on numerous subsequent occasions.

It may have been partly because of his fluency and skill as a debater with would-be debunkers of his ancient "science of the stars" that *Time* dubbed him America's "highbrow astrologer." Crazy he may be, in the judgment of scientific critics, but stupid he isn't.

The first of what was destined to be a long series of debates between Omarr and astronomers over the merits and demerits of astrology came about in June, 1951, when the fledgling astrologer was earning his bread as a reporter and preparing horoscopes as a hobby at night.

He was invited to appear on Philadelphia's radio station WPEN to do battle with famed astronomer Roy K. Marshall, then director of the Fels Planetarium and science editor of the Philadelphia *Evening Bulletin*. Marshall reveled in giving astrologers verbal spankings and had just administered a stinging one to a well-known New York practitioner of the arcane art.

The debate lasted three hours. At the start, as Omarr tells it, Dr. Marshall peered down on his antagonist much as an elephant might contemplate an insect he was about to crush. But under Omarr's jabbing attacks he speedily lost his cool. By the end of the debate, so Omarr says, he, the astrologer, was cool and confident, whereas the as-

13

tronomer was yelling that astrology was damned nonsense as any fool could plainly see. (The transcript of the debate tends to support Omarr's version of it.)

I asked him if there were any signs that scientists are more willing now than in the past to take another look at astrology.

"Well," he said, sipping his third Manhattan, "I think it is true that more people today find it less fashionable to ridicule astrology and more logical to investigate its claims. Astrology, after all, has great significance for many areas, especially communications and medicine."

Communications?

Omarr explained what he meant. RCA, the world's largest communications system, he said, is utilizing astrological principles to forecast transmission-disrupting magnetic storms.

John H. Nelson, an engineer for RCA, apparently studied electromagnetic storms, formerly blamed solely on sun spots, and found them to be highly correlated with the positions of all the known bodies of the solar system. He reports a predictive accuracy of more than 85 percent. The curious thing, says Omarr, is that the methods of prediction this modern scientist uses are similar to those developed by Ptolemy of Alexandria, an astrologer who lived in the second century A.D.

In medicine, Omarr cited a Florida surgeon, Dr. J. Edson Andrews, who made a study of more than one thousand cases and found that the possibility of postoperative hemorrhage is apparently greater during the period of the full moon. Over a three-year period he discovered that 82 percent of cases of severe bleeding occurred between the moon's first and third quarters.

Dr. Andrews threatened "to become a witch and operate on dark nights only, saving the moonlit ones for romance."

"Mainly," said Sydney Omarr, "the medical indications are: Do not operate on that part of the body which the moon is in, or governs, on that day. Say the moon is in Taurus that day; Taurus governs the throat area, so you wouldn't operate on the throat, assuming there was no emergency. And, as Dr. Andrews discovered, do not operate at all during the full moon, unless there is an emergency, for there is more likely to be hemorrhage.

"Another example of the medical use of astrological values concerns the late Dr. Eldon Tice of Methodist Hospital in Los Angeles. He found that more babies were born during a certain phase of the moon than at any other time in the month, and he regulated his maternity staff based on those moon phases.

"He didn't call what he was doing astrology, but that's what it was."

As Omarr explained it, astrology is concerned with time, which is the dynamic element in the universe.

"Were I so inclined I would quote from the Bible," he smiled, "about there being a time to sow and a time to reap, and so on.

"Farmers, of course, know that you plant according to the phases of the moon. And that meat slaughtered during certain phases of the moon tends to have more shrinkage than that slaughtered at other times. People in the lumber business know that the same thing happens with trees. And even metal expands or contracts according to lunar phases."

Quoting Dr. Carl Jung's aphorism, "Everything born at this moment of time has the characteristics of this moment," Omarr maintained that it applies to all human ventures, including the launching of a ship or a business deal, the opening of a play, and even the asking of a question.

"If a person has a serious question, I do a horary chart for the time the question was formed. Horary comes from the Latin word for hour. We do a horoscope based on the time, as if the question were an individual being born at that time. Using this method, it's possible to come up with some strikingly accurate answers.

"For example, I had a radio program in Los Angeles called 'Sydney Omarr's Almanac.' It was very popular, but in spite of that I had an intuitive feeling of trouble ahead. So I cast a horary chart about the future of the show, based on the time I framed the question. The answer indicated that the show was going off the air.

"Within six weeks it did. In fact, astrology shows disappeared from all CBS radio affiliates at the same time. I can only assume that some unwritten anti-astrology taboo was invoked."

Omarr said he developed his passion for stargazing at fourteen, an age when most boys are developing a passion for girls and smoking under the back staircase (*what* they smoke nowadays, to be sure, may be different from what was in vogue in Omarr's day and mine).

After several years as a newsman, he stepped into astrology full-time when the demands for his astrological services became too onerous for him to retain his amateur status. When General Features syndicate offered to handle a daily horoscope written by him, he took the plunge and became a professional astrologer.

Even if one grants a certain plausibility for astrological claims on the basis of individual charts, what can be said for daily newspaper horoscopes? How can a few sentences sum up the prospects for the millions of readers who happen to have the same sign? There are Aries and Capricorns who, while sharing some characteristics, are as different in other respects as night and day.

"Well," said Omarr, "a daily horoscope such as I do is based on a lunar cycle and gives a general forecast for persons born under the same sun sign. Of course, it's not as accurate or as comprehensive as an individual chart. It's like a patent medicine compared to a prescription medicine. The latter is personalized but the first may do you good as far as it goes.

"Actually, I'd suggest that readers keep a diary of the main events that happened to them for two weeks, then compare it to my forecasts for that period. They'll find an interesting correlation."

Omarr was coy when I asked him how much money he made.

"Let's say I'm giving the government much, much too much," he quipped.

When asked if it was in six figures, he admitted: "Well, certainly you can say that."

Omarr's conversation was liberally sprinkled with the names of famous people who believed in astrology—former California governor Goodwin Knight; novelist Henry Miller; pundit and connoisseur of the occult Aldous Huxley; and the great psychiatrist Dr. Carl Jung.

"When I first met Goodwin Knight, while he was lieutenant-governor of California," said Omarr, "he took me into his office and showed me the horoscopes of every politician he dealt with. He was quite a skillful astrologer himself. He reminded me of Theodore Roosevelt who kept his horoscope mounted on a chess board in the White House."

Henry Miller is Omarr's client and friend. Omarr, in turn, is his fervid admirer, having written a book titled *Henry Miller: His World of Urania,* a study of astrological references and motifs in Miller's works. In his fore-

16

word to that book, Miller rhapsodizes about astrology as a kind of frozen poetry that represents a large part of the accumulated wisdom of the race.

In a letter that Henry Miller wrote to Sydney Omarr on March 1, 1955, he said: "Felt I should let you know with what amazing accuracy events have proceeded this past month—a month which was precisely such as you described. . . . Every time I felt at my wit's end I thought of your words—and just waited prayerfully."

Omarr discussed astrology with Aldous Huxley and found that aficionado of the unusual as enthusiastic about horoscopes as he was about mescaline visions, the ancient Chinese method of healing by sticking people with silver needles called acupuncture, and sitting in dark rooms trying to communicate with the dead.

"It was Aldous Huxley," Omarr recalled, "who said to me that 'when you deal with human beings you can never have an exact science.' And that's certainly true of medicine, psychology—and astrology.

"The setting up of the horoscope is scientific because it's based strictly on mathematics and astronomy; but the interpretation is an art."

Omarr never met Carl Jung, but he has done his best to make as many people as possible aware of Jung's sympathy for astrology. It was Jung who suggested a possible explanation of how astrology works, which astrologers quickly seized upon. He proposed a "principle of synchronicity"—a relationship between such things as the positions of the planets and human events based not on cause and effect but on "meaningful coincidence."

Omarr is inclined to agree with Jung's synchronicity theory of how astrology works. He puts it this way: When it is noon in New York City it is possible to say that more people are in restaurants than at any other time of the day. Yet the fact that it's noon doesn't *cause* people to rush out to restaurants. The relationship between the two things is meaningful but noncausal. This is Jung's synchronicity.

"When we as astrologers say that Uranus, the upsetting planet, is associated with earthquakes, this sounds superstitious to the layman. But we are not saying that Uranus causes earthquakes, only that there is a correlation between the two.

"If somebody says, 'But you've got to come up with some explanation,' I point out that there are many things

17

we accept which science hasn't explained. Has science told us what electricity is? Or magnetism? Or dreams?

"A biologist can cut open a brain but he can't tell you where thoughts come from. Nobody knows where thoughts come from.

"Similarly, we as astrologers may not be able to say why and how Uranus is associated with earthquakes but that doesn't discredit the existence of the association."

As Omarr explained it, astrology is not fatalistic. It doesn't make anybody act in a particular way; it merely provides information as to how a person is likely to act at a particular time, and whether it would be advantageous or disadvantageous to him.

"The principle is that astrology can warn you when the traffic light is red but it can't stop you from crossing against the light," he noted.

He told me about a case that illustrated the principle.

A great, world-famous motion picture actress—it would be unethical for me to use her name without her permission—wanted to get out of doing a certain motion picture and asked me what she should do about it. I did a chart and said she should not break her contract, she would still not have to make the motion picture. Now, it took a great deal of faith on her part but she followed my advice.

She went to England and called me from there and said, "I'm here and the motion picture's in progress."

I said, "Don't worry. That motion picture has badly aspected financing and you won't have to make it."

She said, "It has the best financial backing and the picture is under way."

Well, she still had enough faith to go ahead and not break her contract. As it happened, she fell off a horse and injured her back. Because of that she didn't have to make the motion picture. The production company had to bring in another star. They suffered financially. But she didn't have to make the picture and she didn't have to break her contract.

Had she not consulted astrology or me she would have broken her contract and she would have been blamed for everything and sued for all she had.

I asked Omarr if he practiced what he preached by

using astrology in his own life. He said, somewhat ruefully I thought, "Well, things have gone better for me when I have."

His former wife, Geraldine, who runs a charm school, was there. Omarr mentioned that their marriage had been very short-lived but that they were still good friends.

"Actually, I cast a horary chart to see if we should marry," he confided. "It said not to, that the marriage wouldn't work out. But we went ahead anyway."

How good are astrologers, really, at predicting events?

Well, in astrology as in all other types of forecasting, successes tend to be remembered while errors are conveniently forgotten. But Omarr insisted astrologers had done fantastically well, for instance, in predicting the death of President John F. Kennedy. He said that he himself was among those who had made such a prophecy.

"*Editor and Publisher*, which is the bible of the newspaper business, interviewed me before Kennedy's death and I told them of my feelings about his impending death. But I asked the magazine not to publish them because it would have been in terribly poor taste. However, the late Ray Irwin, a columnist for *Editor and Publisher*, did reveal after the tragic event that I had stated Kennedy was going to die in office."

His dire prediction, Omarr explained, was based on the presidential "death cycle" attributed to the "fatal Jupiter–Saturn conjunction." Astrologers say it is no accident that every American president elected in the twenty-year periods following 1840 died in office: namely, William H. Harrison, Abraham Lincoln, James A. Garfield, William McKinley, Warren G. Harding, Franklin D. Roosevelt—and John F. Kennedy. These were the only chief executives to die in office with the exception of Zachary Taylor.

All these presidents, excluding Taylor were elected under the previously mentioned "malefic" conjunction which astrologers blame for all the trouble.

We will return later to further consideration of this so-called presidential "death rhythm."

When I asked Omarr if he could or would make predictions about current political figures, he said that such questions properly belonged to a specialty called mundane astrology, whereas he concentrates not on political trends or world events but on "individual human beings."

However, he did toss off a capsule astrological impression of California Governor Ronald Reagan: "His rise is meteoric—Uranian, astrologically speaking—and he could go all the way to the very top. And then all the way down. Fast."

To illustrate the hazards of prognostication for an astrologer, Omarr cited a prediction he had made about the former chief justice of the U.S. Supreme Court, Earl Warren.

"I predicted that Earl Warren would win the Republican nomination for president because his chart showed that he would get anything he wanted. But he became chief justice instead. He did get what he wanted, but he wanted the chief justice's position, not the presidency. The problem, you see, is interpretation."

As far as social trends are concerned, Omarr predicted a great religious revival—of a new and different sort—starting in 1971.

"The Age of Aquarius really began on February 4, 1962, when there was a great conjunction of planets in Aquarius, the so-called brotherhood sign.

"This, is seems to me, was the real birth of the space age. And in a way our current racial unrest stemmed from that, because it was discovered that brotherhood means more than many of us had popularly thought; it means man's need and desire to be recognized and to be equal.

"At the end of 1970, the violence started to fade as Neptune moved out of Scorpio into Sagittarius.

"There will be a tremendous religious revival, a marriage of religion and science."

How well can an astrologer describe a person based on his birth data?

An answer to this was provided by Sydney Omarr when we both appeared on a Montreal television program in October, 1969. He was asked to give an instant astrological profile of a mystery subject identified only as "a well-known Canadian born in Montreal on October 18, 1919, at 3 A.M."

"When this person was born, Jupiter was rising; therefore, the odds are that he's a politician," Omarr said.

He didn't know he was describing Canadian Prime Minister Pierre Elliot Trudeau.

"This man has great charm," he continued, "the special kind that we call charisma. He would have made, for example, a wonderful society doctor.

"Yet this charm is the very reason some people dislike

20

him intensely, while others, especially women, are devoted to him.

"His chart indicates strongly the intensification of a relationship with the opposite sex in 1970. From this I surmise that he's not married but will marry next year.

"I also see this man in his public role carrying a heavy burden of financial responsibility, particularly in regard to inflationary pressures."

This impromptu mini-profile of Canada's prime minister was so good that I said to Omarr: "Nobody will believe it wasn't fixed."

The prediction about marriage turned out to be at the very least a semi-hit. Trudeau did not marry in 1970, but on March 5, 1971, the fifty-one-year-old bachelor surprised everybody by marrying twenty-two-year-old Margaret Sinclair.

The sorts of things that Omarr does—a few of which I've described—have made some intelligent people take a second look at the "superstition" of astrology. But something else is happening. Astrology is experiencing a rehabilitation among scientists, although usually under a pseudonymn such as "cosmobiology" or, as at M.I.T., "cosmicology."

The main reason for astrology's rescue from the intellectual dustbin is a string of very recent discoveries which tend to give new credence to the traditional astrological claim—that there is a correspondence of some kind between celestial phenomena and terrestrial events.

Even though most of popular astrology is junk and the typical cut-rate horoscope is swindle, a growing number of scientists are at least willing to consider whether or not there is a core of truth to the whole business. It is interesting to reflect on how this came about.

In the ancient world, as historians have pointed out, astrology was universally accepted and was a sort of lingua franca. Scholars of different nations could communicate about astrology because its language was mathematics and astronomy.

The reason's for astrology's decline—which really started in the mid-seventeenth century when it was condemned by the French Academy—are not hard to find.

There was the rise of Copernican astronomy and its heliocentric rather than geocentric universe. As the earth receded from the center of the cosmos to a more modest position among the planets, man's estimate of himself in the scheme of things shrank. The idea that man was in "sympathy" (as the medieval thinkers expressed it) with the most distant star seemed far fetched as the stars moved farther and farther away.

Another reason was the rise of astrophysics, which made the question of the mechanism operative in astrology very problematical. No physical energy was uncovered which could possibly reach us from the heavenly bodies and have the effects astrological influences were supposed to have. These seemed more and more to belong to the realm of discredited, magical effluvia.

Astronomer Harlow Shapely of Harvard put it crisply: "The stars and the planets are too far away to have any effect upon living organisms, and that includes man."

Yet another reason for the decline of astrology was our increasing understanding of the processes which actually shape human beings. With the development of medical psychology, we discovered that it could be low blood sugar, rather than the position of Uranus, that makes a man depressed. And that removing part of his brain will radically change his personality regardless of which star he was born under.

Inherited I.Q., diet, glands, emotions—these, said modern science, and not some faraway star, are what make a man what he is.

The present move toward a reconstruction of astrology on a scientific basis has come about because of a number of converging insights.

Recently a noted astronomer—he is head of the department at a large university—confided to me at a dinner party that he "believes" in astrology. When I asked him why, he mentioned the name Michel Gauquelin.

Gauquelin is a French statistical psychologist, trained at the Sorbonne and now working in the Psychophysiological Laboratory at Strasbourg University. His startling experiments are outlined in two unusual books, *Cosmic Clocks* (New York, Henry Regnery Co., 1967) and *The Scientific Basis of Astrology* (New York, Stein and Day, 1969).

Gauquelin hates astrology as it is generally seen; he considers it a "whore" and a "charlatan." What he is championing is "cosmobiology"—the new science of cosmic rhythms, cycles, or patterns, whichever term you prefer. Much of what he has to say, however, certainly sounds like astrology.

22

In 1956, Gauquelin analyzed twenty-five thousand German, Italian, Belgian, and Dutch birth charts and found that people in certain occupations tended to have been born when particular planets were rising. It was established that people born when Mars appeared at the horizon or had just passed the highest point of its daily course across the sky had a greater tendency to become doctors, athletes, or professional soldiers.

He found similar correlations for other planets. Jupiter governed politicians, clergy, and actors; Saturn, scientists and painters; Venus, musicians; and the moon, writers.

Gauquelin could offer no plausible theory to account for this bizarre correlation. He checked his findings and invited other scientists to do the same. Nobody detected a flaw in his method. The correlation apparently was a statistically valid one.

But what did it mean?

Could some "ray" be the cause? Could it permanently affect the person whose birth coincided with it, so that he was predetermined to become a politician, professional soldier, clergyman, or athlete?

Astrology-hater Gauquelin recoiled from any such notion, which to him suggested that the planets, as in traditional astrology, cast a spell over the person born under their influence. He came up with an ingenious alternative theory.

Instead of the time of birth determining the person's make-up, reasoned Gauquelin, why couldn't it be true that the person's make-up determined the time of his birth?

In other words, a baby is not cut out to be a writer because he is born when the moon is rising; rather, he is born when the moon is rising because he is cut out to be a writer.

Crazy? Gauquelin thought so too, but he liked it better than the first theory. So he tried to check out this hypothesis of "planetary heredity," as he came to call it.

If it is true, he argued, that a child has a predisposition to come into the world under certain cosmic conditions which correspond to his biological constitution, this should hold for the child's parents too. Since the child inherits his make-up from his parents, they ought to have shown a predisposition to be born under the same or similar cosmic conditions as the child.

Gauquelin collected more than fifteen thousand matchings of parents and their children. He found that there was a definite correlation between the birth sky of parents and that of their children. If the father had been born with Jupiter rising, the odds were his son was too.

In other words, it looked as though people "chose" their birth time on the basis of their inherited biological constitution. (It's intriguing to speculate that the "choosing" may suggest consciousness in the human being before birth, as reincarnation researcher, Dr. Ian Stevenson, suggests in the last chapter of this book.)

An observation which supported this conclusion was that the parent-child correlation disappeared if the child's birth had been "induced" rather than natural. If the child was born prematurely—by Caesarean section or the use of drugs—rather than at the time he "chose" to be born, the planetary heredity correlation broke down.

In some ways Gauquelin's theory of planetary heredity seems more, not less, outlandish than the magical effluvia theory. But that may be an argument in its favor.

At any rate, Gauquelin's serious, careful research has played a large part in the swing back toward a reassessment of the central astrological claim that man is attuned to his cosmic environment in sundry, subtle ways. And not only man but other animals, and probably vegetable life too.

The old astrological idea that the moon has a strong influence on behavior is supported by new data.

In 1963, at an international medical conference at the University of London, Dr. E. A. Jannino of Lynn, Massachusetts, presented a paper on "moon madness." He said that modern investigation indicated a change in man's electrical potential twice a month, coinciding with the full and new moons.

"A maladjusted group studied had the highest voltage readings," Dr. Jannino reported.

This confirmed the work of psychiatrist Dr. Leonard Ravitz, formerly of the University of Pennsylvania Medical School, who measured electromagnetic waves emitted by the human body.

"A thirty-four-year-old patient suffering from schizophrenia gave readings reaching their highest level on the day of the new moon," Dr. Ravitz reported. "This was always associated with feelings of pressure in his head.

24

He was dramatically more tense, irritable, and preoccupied at such times."

This ties in with the results of a three-year study of human behavior and lunar phases by the American Institute of Medical Climatology and the University of Pennsylvania Medical School, which was completed in 1961. The study, based on data provided by the Philadelphia police department, showed that cases of murder, rape, arson, and aggravated assault were more common during the periods of the full moon.

Even animal and vegetable life responds to lunar influences.

Professor Frank Brown, a noted biologist at Northwestern University, Evanston, Illinois, discovered that oysters he removed from Long Island Sound and brought to his laboratory in Evanston continued to open and close in their previous rhythm for three weeks. Then they went on a twenty-four hour strike.

When the oysters resumed opening and closing, it was in exact correlation with the position of the moon over Professor Brown's laboratory. Yet the lowly oysters, indoors and under artifical light, apparently could have had no way of knowing when the moon was directly overhead.

In experiments with rats, biologist Brown found that a rat shut in a dark room was twice as active when the moon was below the horizon as when it was above. Yet the rat could not see the moon.

Brown hypothesized that the rat was sensitive to very subtle geophysical changes induced by certain cosmic rhythms. He dubbed this sensitivity a "biological clock" and suggested that all living things, including man, probably possess it to some degree.

There are, for example, certain tropical worms, called palolos, which live in coral rock and emerge only twice a year. Astonishingly, they always come out on the first day in the months of October and November when the moon enters the last quarter. Their timing is so precise that the natives of Fiji and Samoa use them as living calendars.

Who tells these worms the precise time to leave their coral haven? Presumably they, too, are responding to some biological clock attuned to the cosmos around them.

Recent research provides clues as to how the interaction occurs between celestial influences and terrestrial life forms.

In the May 17, 1967, issue of *Technology Week*, NASA scientists stated that planetary positions regulate human behavior more strongly than previously believed. The mechanism for this, they indicated, is a resonance between the alpha waves of the human brain and the fundamental pitch of the geomagnetic field which pulses in accord with changing planetary positions.

Physicist Daniel Cohen in Chicago measured the electromagnetic field created by flexing human muscles. He reported the strength of such a field as one five-hundred millionth part as strong as the magnetic field surrounding the whole earth.

It is known that electromagnetic fields interact and that a change in a strong field—the earth's geomagnetic field—could predictably be reflected in a change within the lesser field generated by human muscles. This phenomenon would obviously relate to the possible mechanism of astrology.

Similarly, biophysicist Robert O. Becker of New York State University has noted that each human body has its own electromagnetic field which interacts with the earth's magnetic field. He suggested that there was "a general relationship of some kind between the whole of the human species and the whole of the electromagnetic phenomenon that engages the sun, other stars, and the galaxies."

In the Knoll Pharmaceutical Company's *Hospital Focus*, February 15, 1965, there was a discussion of the mechanisms by which organisms respond to changes in the earth's geomagnetic field. The authors even use the word "astrology" and consider that, apart from horoscopes as such, the ancient "science of the stars" is vindicated.

Just as the moon impinges invisibly on organisms, so does the sun.

Two medical researchers, G. and B. Dull, studied 24,739 cases of suicide in Copenhagen, Frankfurt, and Zurich from 1928 to 1932. They concluded that suicide waves were correlated with periods of sun spot activity. (Sun spots are tremendous explosions on the surface of the sun, also called "solar flares.")

Dr. Robert Becker, mentioned previously, said in *Newsweek*, May 13, 1963, that he had established a relationship between the number of admissions to psychiatric hospitals and the earth's magnetic activity, which is profoundly affected by son spots.

The theory here seems to be that solar flares cause

changes in the geomagnetic field of the earth, and these in turn cause changes in the electromagnetic fields surrounding individual humans. These changes could produce nervous excitation, or, in the mentally ill, violent outbursts.

A number of doctors have written about so-called meteorotropic disease—illnesses induced by changes in lunar, solar, or other planetary influences. Again, sun spots are usually indicated, precipitating everything from certain heart ailments to premature labor in pregnant women to epidemics of diphtheria, typhus, and other things.

Dr. Maki Takata, a Japanese medical scientist at Tokyo's Toho University, calls man "a living sun dial." He has found that certain characteristic changes in human blood serum correlate with solar flares. In other words, the blood in your veins responds to eruptions on the surface of the sun.

Soviet scientists take the effect of solar radiations on human beings very seriously. More than fifty years ago Dr. A. Chizevsky linked many deaths of sick people to a so-called twenty-seven-day cycle of solar activity.

In the early 1950s, Dr. Vaslav Desyatov of the Tomsk Medical Institute analyzed what he called "killer weather." Using astrophysical measurements and medical statistics, he concluded that the second day after a big sun storm is dangerous, often fatally so, for certain patients.

He theorized that solar storms bombard earth with tremendous streams of radiation which produce violent changes in the magnetic field around the earth; such changes affect all living organisms. Man is particularly vulnerable because of his highly developed, and therefore more sensitive, central nervous system.

Parallel research at the Institute of Cardiology, Moscow, from 1944 to 1966, indicated that a close relationship exists between cardiovascular attacks and solar magnetic storms. And results of research at the Institute of Higher Nervous Activity and Neurophysiology, also in the Soviet capital, showed that strong fluctuations in a magnetic field can cause measurable changes in human brain wave activity which may produce drowsiness or behavioral aberrations.

In 1965 the Soviets established the world's only alarm system to detect magnetic storms. When a solar storm is reported, doctors in many Soviet hospitals take precautionary measures. Most standard treatment of patients

27

with heart or circulatory ailments is temporarily stopped. Some patients receive special drugs. Extra rest periods and sometimes a restricted diet are introduced. Result: A reported definite reduction in post-magnetic storm deaths or relapses.

Where does all this leave us?

Well, as I have said, it makes a strong case for a re-evaluation of astrology—an attempt to prune away the nonsense and mumbo jumbo, retain the insights that are valid, and add new ones contributed by modern science.

Still unanswered is the question of whether astrological phenomena are causal or acausal.

Does the full moon actually cause some mentally disturbed people to become more disturbed? Or does the full moon merely indicate that such a disturbance will occur?

It is tempting to speculate that there is a causal chain linking explosions on the surface of the sun, changes in the earth's magnetic field, and changes in the individual magnetic fields around human beings that produce outbreaks of violence.

But the causal theory seems to break down once you try to apply it to more subtle aspects of human behavior. For example, take the so-called presidential death rhythm which is blamed for the demise in office of presidents elected at twenty-year intervals since 1840. Discussing both causal and acausal views of this phenomenon, psychologist Stanley Krippner of the Maimonides Medical Center, Brooklyn, said:

It is not impossible that the Saturn–Jupiter conjunction affects the electromagnetic fields of certain inhabitants of the planet Earth. Does this permit us to assume, however, a causal relationship between the planetary conjunctions and the periodic deaths of Presidents Harrison, Lincoln, Garfield, McKinley, Harding, Roosevelt, and Kennedy?

If so, we must explain why some of these presidents died from disease and others from assassins' bullets. We must also explain, in causal terms, why this bizarre phenomenon affects the United States rather than another of the Earth's political subdivisions. . . .

These problems tax our powers of logic and analysis so heavily that it is tempting to favor an acausal explanation. Carl Jung postulated that events could

28

be either causal or acausal in nature. Thus, the complexity of the link between the Saturn–Jupiter conjunction and U.S. presidential deaths may indicate that these cycles are but connected bits of the same synchronous event. . . .

Causal or acausal?
Like "To be or not to be," this is the question. The search for an answer goes on.

In the meantime, what Harold Urey, the cosmochemist and one of today's most distinguished physical scientists, said about the astrological convictions of such historical worthies as Copernicus, Kepler, and Newton is significant: "What interested minds like theirs just can't be nonsense. . . ."

THREE

The Power of Desuggestion

To plunge from the stars into the human unconscious is not such a long journey, really. Both outer space and inner space contain profound enigmas, none more important than the staggering powers of the mind, impatient to be unlocked. . . .

THE MOST potent medicine is faith.

This was the conclusion of Dr. Alfred J. Kantor, a distinguished proctologist (specialist in rectal diseases), after investigating a new drug.

Dr. Kantor, president emeritus of the Academy of Psychosomatic Medicine and one time editor of the *American Journal of Proctology*, was asked to evaluate a treatment for benign rectal diseases that had been used in Europe but was unknown in the United States. He employed what is commonly called the double-blind method.

The physicians doing the clinical tests under Dr. Kantor's direction were sent two medications that looked exactly alike, the ingredients of which were unknown both to them and their patients. One contained the new drug; the other was a placebo—dummy medication—and contained only milk sugar.

"The interesting fact," reported Dr. Kantor in the January, 1959, issue of *Science of Mind*, "was that the placebo proved to be even more effective than the supposedly active combination of drugs!"

Indeed, one of the doctors said that his sister had suffered from rectal disease for many years and this was the first medication to give her relief. He was eager to know the nature of the drug.

"It was my duty to write and tell him that the medication was only milk sugar," recounted Dr. Kantor. "It was purely a placebo effect."

The milk sugar had no inherent medicinal properties; the woman had been healed by her own belief.

Actually, noted Dr. Kantor, no medication—not even the most pharmacologically potent—can be separated from the placebo effect, which may be negative as well as positive.

"The most 'active' drugs can become relatively inactive in the hands of a physician who is not held in sufficient esteem by the patient," he observed, "and a relatively 'inactive' or even inert preparation may become highly potent when administered by a very authoritative physician."

Data on the placebo effect were summarized by Dr. Bernard Grad, a biologist in the psychiatry department at McGill University, Montreal, in *Corrective Psychiatry and Journal of Social Therapy*, Volume 12, 1966.

"A recent comprehensive review . . . reported that 40.6 percent of 14,177 patients with illnesses ranging from simple headache to multiple sclerosis obtained relief from placebo pills," said Dr. Grad.

He cited a case in which the placebo effect reversed the normal pharmacological action of a drug. A man was given atropine sulfate, believing it to be the same drug he had previously received. The previous drug was prostigmine which, as expected, had induced abdominal cramps, diarrhea, and extreme stomach acidity. The atropine sulfate had exactly the same effect on the man, although it normally has the opposite effect!

Even more puzzling, in a way, is the influence of the investigator's personality when he has no bias about the drug being tested.

Grad cited the case of two investigators who were asked to measure gastric secretions in healthy humans in response to pill X. It was a placebo but the investigators weren't told this; nor were they told how to expect the pill to act.

Curiously, their results differed wildly. One investigator reported that his subjects showed a 12 percent increase in gastric acidity; the other measured an 18 percent *decrease* in his subjects. The differing results were consistent whenever these particular experimenters were used.

Stranger still was the case in which a doctor's mistaken faith apparently made a placebo effective and a pharmacologically active drug ineffective.

The patient in this case had suffered from intractable asthma for twenty-seven years. During this time he built up a tolerance to epinephrine, a drug commonly used to relieve acute bronchial spasms. In his desperation to find another remedy, the patient made himself readily available as a guinea pig to test new drugs.

Finally, one just-on-the-market pharmaceutical product provided dramatic relief. When he was given this drug he was asthma-free; when it was stopped, the symptoms promptly returned. The patient's doctor wanted to test the placebo effect so he substituted sugar pills, which the pharmaceutical company had also sent, without the man's knowledge. Immediately, as the doctor had expected, the asthmatic symptoms returned.

There were several switches from drug to placebo and back again—all yielding results consistent with the doctor's expectations. Finally, he was satisfied that the objective value of the drug to his patient had been demonstrated beyond doubt.

Then he reported to the pharmaceutical company and found, to his bewilderment, that inadvertently he had confused the drug with the placebo. The patient all along had been responding to the sugar pill.

What happened here?

The doctor had been careful not to reveal to the patient anything about the medication he was receiving. As far as the patient was concerned, all the pills were the same. Yet the placebo, which the doctor mistakenly believed was the real drug, worked consistently and the drug didn't.

The doctor's belief must have transmitted itself to the patient, suggested Bernard Grad, either directly or indirectly. Perhaps the doctor's faith adhered, as it were, to the placebo pill, in the same way that psychic impressions are claimed by clairvoyants to cling to a personal object. Or perhaps the patient picked up the doctor's faith from unconscious clues—possibly even by telepathy.

Just as the patient's faith in his physician is an important factor in his recovery, a negative transference between patient and doctor may not only slow down or prevent recovery but may make the patient worse. This is especially evident in psychotherapy, Grad said.

He cited studies indicating that although some mentally and emotionally ill persons showed a definite improvement with certain therapists, other patients deteriorated during therapy, ending up in poorer health than they might have been without treatment.

"While good therapists tend to produce better psychological functioning," Grad said, "bad ones tend to produce further regressive behavior."

It is not so much formal training as enthusiasm that counts in a psychotherapist, coupled with a genuine, deeply felt desire and confidence that the patient will get well. Studies have indicated that people with no training in psychotherapy, but with empathy and the capacity for involvement, have achieved better results than qualified therapists.

Group therapy was conducted with 295 institutionalized psychotics, Grad reported. One bunch was treated by undergraduate college students with no formal background in psychotherapy; the other received treatment from professionals. The results of therapy were measured by before-and-after psychological testing of the patients. The group treated by the students scored better in terms of improved mental health than the other group.

Grad speculated that possibly "the untrained personnel were taken by the novelty of the task" and this accounted for the difference. To test this theory, he suggested that the same students be used in several successive experiments of this kind.

The crucial fact about any doctor-patient relationship, Grad concluded, is that suggestion, whether overt or not, plays a dynamic part.

Someone may say here: "Well, what about it? This isn't new. Most people nowadays know about placebos. There's no mystery. Simply the power of suggestion."

The power of suggestion.

These four words are used by some scientists as a sort of incantation to conjure away many unexplained phenomena.

An unusual, totally unexpected recovery? Nothing to get excited about; it's merely the power of suggestion (or, that other stock phrase to explain away the unexplained, "spontaneous remission").

The word suggestion is similar to the word gravity; both are widely used and both are labels often mistaken for explanations.

When someone says, "What goes up must come down because of the law of gravity," all he's really saying is that it must come down because it must come down. Sheer tautology.

No one knows yet what gravity *is;* no one has observed the hypothetical particle called a graviton. The idea of gravity, therefore, although useful, does not explain anything.

The same is true with suggestion. To declare that milk sugar ointment healed a long-standing rectal disease by the power of suggestion doesn't shed any light on the why of it. Precisely how does suggestion work? By what mechanisms? Why can sheer belief—a state of mind—relieve long-standing asthma or reverse the known action of a drug?

What really is this mysterious power of suggestion?

Hypnosis is a form of suggestion, possibly the most powerful form. In hypnosis the censor of the conscious mind is bypassed and suggestions are fed directly into the deep mind. Some of the results can be astonishing.

The *British Medical Journal* of August, 1952, reported the case of a sixteen-year-old boy with icthyosis—a congenital, disfiguring, incurable skin disease—who was treated by a London physician, Dr. Albert Abraham Mason, using hypnotherapy. Over several weeks of hypnotic treatment 90 percent of the boy's body affected by the icthyosis cleared. The boy was taught self-hypnosis to maintain the improvement.

Dr. Robert W. Laidlaw, former chief of psychiatry at New York's Roosevelt Hospital, has said: "I have no way of proving this, but I have a definite feeling that there is some estrasensory or parapsychological factor in hypnosis."

In other words, when you look deeply enough into the phenomenon of suggestion it has a large element of the unexplained.

Recently I met a Bulgarian psychiatrist, Dr. Georgi Lozanov, who has devised a spectacularly successful self-help technique which he calls suggestology, "the science of suggestion." My introduction to him came through mutual friends, Shiela Ostrander and Lynn Schroeder, who describe suggestology in their stimulating book, *Psychic Discoveries Behind the Iron Curtain* (New York, Prentice-Hall, 1970). Dr. Lozanov was in North America to discuss his methods with American and Canadian scholars.

According to this scientist—a handsome, charming man in his forties, with wavy, slightly receding hair—his research started with the very question I have raised: What is the power of suggestion?

He noted that many of his colleagues, when confronted with a puzzling mental or medical phenomenon, murmured the nonexplanation: "Suggestion."

"I decided to look into this so-called suggestion," he said, "to try to discover just what it is and exactly how it works."

Lozanov brought to his investigation a background of more than twenty-five years of yoga study, boht in Europe and India. He reached the conclusion that suggestion, or the "suggestive state," was the key to the unusual feats of some yogis.

He said he also discovered that what releases the greatest untapped potential of the mind is "the power of *de*-suggestion."

"My technique of suggestology is different from hypnosis," he said in his precise, almost unaccented English (which he told me he taught himself in six weeks, using his own methods).

"Hypnosis is a sleeplike state in which there is a limitation of perception. Suggestion, on the other hand, is a state of full connection with the environment.

"Actually, we don't suggest; we desuggest.

"All of us are bombarded constantly with limiting suggestions. We are conditioned to believe that we can only remember so much, that we are bound to be sick, that there are rigid limits to what we can achieve. The purpose of suggestology is to free people from these limitations of thinking imposed on them by the process of negative conditioning to which we're all exposed."

Using suggestology, said Dr. Lozanov, most psychosomatic diseases could be cured. The principle is not to attack specific symptoms but to saturate the unconscious with suggestions of well-being that counteract the conditioning by which most people have come to accept sickness as normal, natural, and inevitable.

As important as the healing of existing diseases, said the apostle of suggestology, is the establishment of "a prophylactic mental atmosphere" to prevent people from succumbing to new emotionally induced symptoms.

Applied to education, as "suggestopedia," the Lozanov method can speed up the learning process as much as fifty times, he claimed. An utter beginner could acquire a working knowledge of French, German, Greek, or any other European language in a month. Presumably, learning Sanskrit or Cantonese might take a little longer.

"People can learn one hundred fifty to two hundred words per lesson," Lozanov said, "once the antisuggestive barriers are removed."

These claims struck some critics as exaggerated and Lozanov was challenged. An official scientific commission was appointed by the Bulgarian government to study suggestology in its application to learning. Apparently it received a clean bill of health. In 1966 the Bulgarian Ministry of Education established a center for suggestopedia in Dr. Lozanov's state-supported Institute of Suggestology in Sofia.

The essence of suggestopedia seems to be distraction. In a typical class, as Lozanov described it, the students sit quietly while soft music—Beethoven, Brahms—is piped in. Over the music the voice of a teacher, with varying speed and intonation, repeats, say, words and phrases in French. The students don't appear to be listening to the teacher; as a matter of fact, they've been warned not to.

"Relax. Don't think about anything. Listen only to the music." This is Dr. Lozanov's formula for painless learning.

Again, he says, the secret is desuggestion. The quiet, relaxed mood and the absorption in the music eases and dissolves the tensions, stresses, and anxieties which normally hamper the learning process. As people learn to enter more deeply into this "free state of consciousness"—actually, a condition of alert nonthinking—they find that their ability to absorb and retain new material is enormously increased.

Lozanov insists that human memory has an almost limitless potential and, like a sponge, constantly expands so that the more it soaks up the more it can soak up. But first the memory must be freed, by desuggestion, from the false ideas of limitation which chain it.

Suggestology has other applications. One of the most dramatic is in controlling bodily functioning. Anything that hypnosis can do, says Lozanov, suggestology can do. And, unlike hypnosis, it works with anybody and raises no legal or psychological problems.

Consider what Lozanov calls "thought anesthesia."

On August 24, 1965, the first major surgery on a patient anesthetized by suggestology took place in Bykovo, Bulgaria. It was filmed and has been seen by numerous medical scientists.

The patient was a fifty-year-old gym instructor with an inguinal hernia, a condition requiring major and complex surgery. The operation was expected to take an hour.

During that time the patient was to receive no anesthesia except the suggestions used by Dr. Lozanov. The two met for several conditioning sessions prior to the surgery.

As nurses wheeled the patient into the operating room, Dr. Lozanov, walking beside him, began his suggestions.

The surgeons made an incision through the skin and muscle. The patient felt nothing, was fully conscious, and talked normally to the operating team.

As the surgery progressed, Lozanov told the patient to suggest to himself that circulation to the area of the incision would decrease to control bleeding. There was very little loss of blood. The operation ended with the patient suggesting to himself that the wound would heal rapidly and without infection. This, too, transpired.

Lozanov insists that this was not hypnosis. However, without making an issue out of terminology—he agrees that hypnosis and suggestology are related phenomena— it is a fact that a subject in a state of "waking hypnosis" would behave exactly as Lozanov's patient reportedly did. Such a subject would appear to be perfectly normal— certainly not asleep—and yet have the power to reduce or cancel pain perception in part or all of his body.

Experts in hypnosis, such as Dr. George Estabrooks, former head of the psychology department at Colgate University, have pointed out that the somnambulistic subject can be trained to act as though he weren't hypnotized and defy detection by the sharpest-eyed observer.

The important point about Dr. Lozanov's report, at any rate, isn't whether suggestology or waking hypnosis was involved but that the patient, using his mind alone, was able to control pain during major surgery.

An interesting confirmation of Lozanov's claim that suggestion can do anything hypnosis can comes from the research of an American psychologist, Dr. Theodore Xenophon Barber. Over several years he has published his findings that suggestion alone, without inducing any trance, can cause positive and negative hallucinations, analgesia, release of buried memories, and other phenomena generally attributed to hypnosis.

Lozanov's concept of "desuggestion," and what might be called resuggestion, is echoed by an American Episcopal priest-psychologist who is one of today's most adventurous trailblazers in hypnotherapy. Canon Joseph Wittkofski, referring to the way in which he has been able to help juvenile delinquents with very severe behavioral problems, says: "The teen-ager must first be *dehypnotized*. He must be freed from early destructive conditioning. Then he can be hypnotized into new and worthwhile behavior patterns."

My friend, Canon Wittkofski, puts his congregations to sleep. Deliberately, that is.

Combining Mesmer with Jesus, he has produced changes in people's lives which some regard as almost miraculous: for example, a crippled arthritic woman walking without her crutches after several hypnotic sessions; a teen-aged girl with a history of academic disasters leading her class; or a man ravaged by a monumental gastric ulcer and a lifelong allergy to milk getting relief from both.

Canon Wittkofski, a husband and father in his fifties, is no crank Svengali. He was a college instructor in psychology, served two terms as chaplain of the Pennsylvania State Senate, and was praised by his bishop, Rt. Rev. Austin Pardue of Pittsburgh (now retired), as a "genius" with a singular gift for helping and healing people.

"Reverend Joseph Wittkofski has been a close friend of mine for over twenty years," said Bishop Pardue, "and I have found him to be one of the most brilliant men I have been privileged to meet.

"People flock to him from far and wide for counsel, spiritual direction, and psychological therapy. He has never publicized himself, since people have told one another of their good fortune through his ministry."

Many of those who seek help from the priest-hypnotist are sent by their doctors. He only uses hypnosis in a profoundly religious setting, as a tool of faith.

Every Good Friday, during the service in St. Mary's Church in Charleroi, Pennsylvania, near Pittsburgh, where he has been parish priest for twenty-five years, Canon Wittkofski hypnotizes his congregation into deeper faith.

Standing in the pulpit, he holds aloft a crucifix with a silver corpus. He asks every person in the pews to fix his eyes upon the crucifix.

"And as you watch it," he intones, in his even, mellow, infinitely reassuring voice, "the crucifix is growing larger and larger, filling the whole church. . . . And you are getting drowsier . . . your eyes are closing . . . and you are at Calvary. . . You are approaching the cross on which Christ hangs"

Then, with the congregation in at least a light trance ("fully 90 percent go under"), Wittkofski re-creates for them the events of the first Good Friday. It is as if time has run backwards, with Christ again being crucified and buried, and then resurrected.

"For everybody there," says Canon Wittkofski, "this is a profound religious experience which deepens and enriches their faith and love for God and man."

Hypnotizing a congregation?

Yes, some find the idea—well, strange is one word. But Wittkofski is unfazed by criticism. He treats it as a parent might the intellectual deficiencies of a child—with good-humored tolerance.

"Hypnosis," he avers with evangelical fervor, "is a form of deep meditation, or what I call total prayer. It provides a way of implanting positive, health-giving suggestions in the individual's unconscious mind."

Hypnosis probably had a religious origin, he maintains, in the "temple sleep" of ancient Egypt some five thousand years ago. The sick person was permitted to sleep in the god's chamber and during his repose—trance, really—the healing deity appeared in a vision for which the pilgrim had been psychologically prepared through the practice of certain religious exercises. The vision, and the recovery which usually followed, were hypnotic phenomena, says Wittkofski.

"Historically, hypnosis is a religious not a medical phenomenon," he declared. Wittkofski interprets many biblical passages, including the miracles of Christ, in terms of hypnotic experience.

"The words of Solomon, 'I sleep but my heart waketh,' are nothing but a bit of poetry for most people, but hypnosis is clearly what's being described.

"In the vision of Peter with reference to Cornelius (Acts 10: 1–22), Peter's praying is explicitly connected with his falling into a trance and having a vision. The word trance is used. More hypnosis.

"And Christ's Transfiguration, one of the most dramatic episodes in the New Testament, indicates that here Jesus used his knowledge of religious hypnotism.

"Jesus, the Bible says, 'took Peter and John and James and went up into a mountain to pray.' The apostles passed into a trancelike state, since 'Peter and they that were with him were heavy with sleep.' But like common hypnotic experience this was waking sleep.

39

"The voice from the cloud, which the apostles heard, was more hypnotic experience; it served to widen their understanding of the nature of Christ."

Jesus, suggests Canon Wittkofski, was the world's greatest mesmerist; he hypnotized people out of their sins and sicknesses and into a new way of life.

The priest said he turned to hypnosis as a means of helping people following an incident in his early ministry thirty years ago.

"A desperate man came to me," he recalled. "After having suffered a grave mental disorder, he had been released from the hospital. Although he was rational, his personality conflict remained unresolved. In an attempt to help him I used every standard procedure of pastoral counseling. And then he went out and hanged himself— still clutching a small crucifix that I had given him.

"This tragedy made me realize that to give real help to disturbed people I must be able to attack their problems on the level at which they exist, in the deep mind. Hypnosis beckoned."

Though he cautions that religion-oriented suggestion is not magic or a cure-all, and that only men with proper training and motivation should use it, Canon Wittkofski admits to being more audacious in its use than the typical medical or scientific hypnotist. He calls this "the practice of hypnosis in unexplored areas." Some of his results seem to come straight out of the unexplained.

One of his early cases was a young woman in his parish who suffered from greatly impaired kidney function. In the days before artificial kidneys or transplants, her life expectancy was very limited. So "Father Joe," as his parishioners called him, tried something frankly experimental on the premise that a woman with no hope had nothing to lose.

"After our first session," he recalled, "the woman's mental outlook underwent a remarkable change. Her pain diminished. She noticed that things she held in her hand grew salty, which possibly indicated that skin excretion was partly compensating for the kidney breakdown. When the specialist who had been treating her noticed the radical improvement in her condition she told him about the hypnotic sessions.

"The doctor said, 'I've never heard hypnosis recommended for diseased kidneys but you tell Father Joe that I'm with him 100 percent.'"

The woman lived for several years (instead of the prophesied six months), married, and then died of something other than kidney disease.

In another case, Jack, a "bedraggled, woeful-looking man," shuffled into Canon Wittkofski's hypnotic parlor. He had been referred by his doctor. He was suffering from a daunting array of afflictions, including depression, insomnia, a stomach ulcer, and an allergy to milk.

"The doctor has ordered me to drink as much milk as possible for my ulcer," he wailed, "and I can't stand milk. It makes me sick. I bring it up. Always have."

The priest put Jack in a trance and gave him reassuring suggestions of the presence and love of God. (These provide the foundation, Wittkofski says, for the therapy to follow.) Then he began probing for the cause of the milk allergy. Using age regression, he traced it back to an incident when Jack was two years old and his stern father forced the child to drink some milk that he didn't want.

"It was wild," Canon Wittkofski recollected. "In the trance, Jack, a grown man, kicked and screamed as he had when he was a baby. I was sure I had found the root trauma.

"The fact is, you see, that if you force a child to do something he doesn't want to do, he usually retaliates by getting sick. This is what happened to Jack. Ever since that incident at the age of two, milk had made him throw up. I removed the allergy in a few minutes by explaining to Jack, while he was in the trance, that he had outgrown his childish reaction and from now on would be able to drink milk and enjoy it. He did."

Reminiscent of Georgi Lozanov's suggestopedia is Canon Wittkofski's hypnotic work with slow learners. He cited one case as a classic example of how deep suggestion can unlock learning potential.

A teen-aged girl, who had been an unwanted orphan since early childhood, desperately wished to become a nurse. But her high school record was deplorable. She took the examination for entrance to nursing school three times and each time flunked more resoundingly than on the previous occasion. Finally, she was told not to apply again.

Canon Wittkofski took up the girl's cause, with not a few misgivings, he allows. He pleaded with the hospital superintendent and the girl was admitted provisionally as a personal favor to him. During the weeks before she started the course he worked with her many hours, using hypnosis to build self-esteem, heighten alertness, and improve memory.

The result: The girl finished her nurse's training near the top of her class.

As the man who believes that total faith can make a molehill out of a mountain, Canon Wittkofski has had many mentally ill persons who have not responded to medical treatment referred to him. Some of them have responded to his brand of religion-oriented hypnotherapy. (For a full discussion of religion and hypnosis, see *The Pastoral Use of Hypnotic Technique*, by the Reverend Joseph Wittkofski, Springfield, Illinois, Charles C. Thomas Publisher, 1971.)

Wittkofski has his own theory about the cause of much mental illness.

"I am more and more convinced," he said, "that mental illness not resulting from disease, injury, or malformation is induced by autohypnosis. People hypnotize themselves into a state of depression, anxiety, inadequacy, or suppressed rage, with all the physical complications these things can produce.

"The cure is de-hypnotizing them, liberating them from the faulty thought patterns which constrict them, and implanting new, positive thought patterns.

"The word 'repent,' used so frequently in the Bible, really means 'to change one's mind.' The way to improved well-being is by changing one's mind, at the deepest level."

Canon Wittkofski once remarked to me that he would be willing to try hypnosis as a last resort in cases of terminal malignancy. He said he was sure it could deaden the pain, and might do more.

"Such as regress the tumor?" I asked.

"Why not?" he replied. "The tumor is fed by a blood supply from the body. Isn't it feasible that hypnosis, properly used, might be able to shut down those blood vessels and starve the tumor to death?"

The idea, as any doctor will tell you, is far out. But interestingly, Dr. George Estabrooks, in the April, 1971, issue of *Science Digest*, referred to the significant success of New Jersey physician Howard Miller in hypnotically regressing tumors in a dozen inoperable cancer patients.

The notion of cancer being treated by hypnosis becomes more credible in the light of recent insights into the emotional factors in the development of the disease. Two psychologists, Dr. Claus Bahnson of Eastern Pennsylvania Psychiatric Institute, and Dr. George Solomon of Stanford University, have outlined the personality of the cancer-prone person. He turns out to be the typical "nice guy," who never lets his feelings of anger and annoyance show, tends to make a fetish of discipline, and is a bit of a square.

The way mothers raise their children and teach them how to cope with their emotions may determine whether those children in later life will develop cancer, the two researchers told the American Cancer Society's science writers' seminar in Phoenix in April, 1971.

Psychologist Bahnson said failure in a job, the death of a loved one, or loss of self-esteem in any of a dozen different ways may trigger cancer in people who have never learned to express their emotions openly and honestly.

Dr. Solomon said that emotional stress may affect body hormones which, in turn, affect the body's immune system. The immune or defense system may be able to ward off cancer until such emotional stress weakens it.

What happens in a typical hypnotic or "prayer-therapy" (as he sometimes calls it) session in Canon Wittkofski's study?

The subject has many faces. She may be a middle-aged woman with migraine headaches, or an elderly woman with crippling, painful arthritis. He may be an asthmatic teen-aged boy who yearns to make the football team, a businessman with a whopping ucler, a housewife with morbid fears, or a young husband who's sexually impotent. Possibly he or she is a clergyman who has lost his faith in a welter of emotional confusion, a respectable woman hooked on sleeping pills, or just a so-so student looking for help in improving his grades.

The subject settles down in a comfortable chair. Canon Wittkofski puts on a record of soft, soothing music. Then he asks the person to gaze into the eyes of a painting of Christ on the wall—eyes which are deep set and of infinite sadness.

"As you look into the Savior's eyes," the priest intones in his languorous voice, "you will feel a deep peace flowing through you. You will sink into a peaceful sleep in which you will feel enveloped in the love of God."

When the subject enters the hypnotic state—which may take two minutes or half an hour—Canon Wittkofski embarks on a process of reprogramming the deep mind where attitudes are formed.

"You will go into yourself, for Jesus said, 'the kingdom of God is within you.' You let go completely and let God. . . .

"Prayer can make and keep you well. . . . Your eyes feel cool and comfortable. . . . You feel surrounded by the presence of God in whom you live and move and have your being. . . . Your body is totally relaxing now. . . . You are being saturated with the consciousness of the presence of God.

"Outside matters lose their power to distract you as you sink deeper and deeper into the consciousness of God. . . . As you grow fruitfully passive in the presence of God, you grow more responsive to the spirit of God.

"You find a sense of joy and peace spreading through you. . . . Turn your thinking now to positive thoughts for the renewal of your body. Think of the promise of Christ, 'Lo, I am with you always'. . . ."

The reason his method often works when others don't, says the priest-hypnotist, is the tremendous emotional power of such archetypes as God, Christ, and the Holy Spirit. These symbols seem to touch the depths of human personality and release the most dynamic forces latent there.

Other, doubtless even deeper, dimensions of the healing phenomenon are explored in Chapter Five.

PART II

Into Deeper Waters:
Beyond Time and Space

FOUR

Plants Have a Love Life Too

If man has hidden depths within him, what about other living things? Plants, even? There is startling evidence that thoughts, feelings, maybe even something akin to a soul, lurk in the lowly philodendron. . . .

GEORGE BERNARD SHAW, who was a fanatical vegetarian, used to call meat eaters "the living graves of dead animals."

Well, there's bad news for such vegetarians in a new scientific report—plants apparently can perceive love and pain and become emotionally involved with their owners.

This, at least, is the contention of New Yorker Cleve Backster, an ebullient, middle-aged authority on the use of the polygraph, or lie detector. (He has served as polygraph consultant to the Central Intelligence Agency—in fact he instituted its polygraph examination program, which is still being used—and in 1951 he founded the Backster School in New York, the first nonmilitary institution to conduct advanced courses in polygraph techniques.)

Recently I heard Cleve Backster describe his off-the-beaten-track research, and I discussed it with him.

Many of his findings intermesh neatly with data independently reported by other researchers. Such a similarity strongly suggests an objective reality to the claims, and they have far-reaching implications.

The following are highlights of Backster's claims:

1. Plants are capable of "primary perception" and appear to have "emotions."
2. Plants apparently monitor the thoughts and feelings of humans in their immediate environment.
3. There appears to be a communications system

among all living things which operates at the cellular level.

4. This communications network functions independently of space and possibly time.

5. Plants, and probably all living things however primitive, appear to possess memory and to be capable of at least rudimentary learning.

Let us consider in detail Cleve Backster's work and discover why the "Backster effect" is already part of the parlance of parapsychology.

In normal use, the polygraph works by detecting the human subject's emotional reactions to questions as indicated by changes in his bodily functioning. One device measures breathing rate and blood pressure. Another, and this is the one Backster uses on plants, measures what is called the "galvanic skin response." Traditionally, this has been attributed to changes in the electrical resistance of the person's skin due to perspiration stimulation. Backster, however, who has spent twenty-three years studying the galvanic skin response, says that perspiration now is discounted as the crucial causal factor. But at any rate, there is "a shift in the person's electrical potential," as he puts it, "which causes the pen tracing the polygraph recording to go up and down in relation to the person's emotional state."

If a guilty subject is interrogated about a crime, any question bearing on his guilt normally elicits what polygraphists call "a threat-to-well-being response"—the pen, tracing wiggly lines on a graph, makes a sudden dramatic leap, or, in polygraphese, "an excursion." It is by examining the pattern of such emotional peaks that the operator forms a judgment about the subject's guilt or innocence.

By attaching the electrodes of a polygraph to the leaves of plants, says Cleve Backster, he has gotten tracings which resemble those of the galvanic skin response in humans. Or, to put it more technically: "We have found a configuration, so far as electronic instrumentation is concerned, that represents what is transpiring within the living plant."

Backster calls this "evidence of the existence of a perception capability in plant life."

Before you dismiss Mr. Backster as being as potted as his plants, you should consider that his research is scrupulously documented, has been reported respectfully in such serious publications as *Medical World News* and the

International Journal of Parapsychology, and he told me, has been well-received by scientific audiences from coast to coast.

Most significant of all, his findings have been substantially duplicated by other researchers. Professor E. Douglas Dean of the Newark College of Engineering, former president of the Parapsychological Association (the professional organization for ESP researchers), told me that he had confirmed Backster's work in preliminary trials. And psychiatrist Dr. Aristide Esser of the research center at Rockland State Hospital in Orangeburg, New York, also has duplicated Backster's findings.

"When I first heard about Backster's experiments I laughed it off," Dr. Esser confessed. "I've had to eat my words."

In case you are wondering how Cleve Backster came to hook a lie detector up to a plant in the first place—well, that's a good question.

"Really, I don't know why I did it," he said. "I just had a compulsion to try it. It was an accident, if there's really any such thing.

"Mind you, I did make up a cover story after the event. I had just watered the plant and, since a leaf should make a better electrical conductor when moisture arrives, I decided to say that I attached the electrodes to the leaf to measure the rate of moisture absorption by the plant. But as I say, I concocted that story later."

The date of the event was February 1, 1966. The plant involved was a *Dracaena massangeana*, a type of philodendron. Backster says that he had never owned a plant in his life. This philodendron, and a rubber plant, had been put in the office by his secretary, who picked them up at some sort of greenhouse clearance sale.

After giving in to his strange impulse and attaching the polygraph electrodes to the philodendron leaf, Backster was bemused to notice a humanlike tracing on the graph. The pattern was similar to that of a human subject experiencing mild emotional stimulation of short duration.

Intrigued now, Backster wondered how he could provoke a stronger reaction, if such a thing were possible. He decided to try to elicit a threat-to-well-being response from the philodendron. How? He took one of its leaves and dunked it in a cup of coffee. No reaction.

Then he thought: "I know. I'll get some matches and burn a leaf."

At that precise instant, said Backster, the pen almost jumped off the paper.

"The moment the imagery of fire, of burning that plant, came into my mind," he recalled,

the pen leaped and went into this wild excitation which, in a human, would indicate panic bordering on hysteria.

Now, being scientifically trained, I didn't jump to the conclusion, gee whiz, this plant just read my mind! But I was very intrigued. The plant had appeared to show sentience or a type of consciousness.

I wasn't about to run out of my office into Times Square and shout, "My plant's a mindreader!" and be scooped up in a net. However, I certainly wasn't going to quietly forget what had happened or sweep it under the rug just because it didn't make sense in today's scientific terms.

I waited until my associate came to the office and asked him to attach the electrodes to the plant. He made the same observations.

Then we tried it elsewhere, in Los Angeles and other places across the country, and even in Lebanon, half a world away. The plants over there did the same thing.

The next question was: Will it work with more than one kind of plant? We tried some thirty varieties. Our conclusion was that all kinds of vegetation show a meaningful tracing.

For the next two-and-a-half years, said Backster, a great deal of observing and monitoring of plants took place in an attempt to find out how far their perception extended, and precisely what sort of events they were able to pick up. This period yielded some findings almost as strange as the initial one.

"I found," said Backster,

that when I poured leftover hot water out of the coffee pot down the sink, plants sixty feet away gave a violent polygraph reaction. At first this baffled me.

Then I realized that bacteria had started to accumulate in the sink and the hot water was killing them,

49

and it was this, the death of a life form, to which the plants were reacting. Plants, then, we discovered, are sensitive to the death of cell life in their immediate environment.

One day I cut my finger and put iodine on it. The instant the iodine touched my finger, the plant reacted. I was killing some human cells.

I noticed that when I took a jar of yogurt and jam out of the refrigerator and started to turn the jam into the yogurt with a spoon, the plants reacted. I discovered that some sort of chemical is put in the jam as a preservative and apparently when this chemical, turned up by my spoon, hit the living yogurt cells, killing them, the termination of even the lowly yogurt cells was being picked up by the plants.

At this stage Cleve Backster called in scientists representing a variety of disciplines—chemistry, physics, biology, psychology—and sought their advice in setting up a controlled experiment. At their suggestion he made additional observations.

"One thing we noticed was that the same plant reacted to the death of life forms at least three or four times and then an adaptation took place. The plant stopped reacting. This was very interesting because it suggested that the plant had memory. If the plant doesn't continue to react in a 'neurotic' manner to death in its vicinity this seems to mean that it remembers that nothing happened to it the last time this occurred so there's no need to get upset again."

A carefully designed experiment was set up, based on the plants' apparent reception of some signal from living things in their immediate environment at the moment of death.

The type of cell life chosen was brine shrimp, miniscule creatures which fish love to eat.

"One reason for picking them was that there's no Society for the Prevention of Cruelty to Brine Shrimp," Cleve Backster said with a wry grin. "You have to be very careful in biological research, you know, because you can get into all kinds of trouble if you use animal life. Thus far I've received only one why-are-you-killing-those-poor-brine-shrimp letter."

From observation, Backster and his co-workers had discovered that if humans were around they appeared to "jam" the signals from such tiny things as brine shrimp—the plants tuned out the shrimp and tuned in the people. So the experiment had to be fully automated, with no human present.

Also, it had been noticed that if the shrimp were unhealthy there appeared to be no signal transmitted on their termination. This might suggest that a lowering of the organism's vitality reduced or canceled the signal. But Backster had a different interpretation.

"Maybe it means that if there was some kind of preparation for demise, if the shrimp knew they were dying, if you like, and had given up, they didn't do a thing when they died, as far as there being a signal."

At any rate, only healthy brine shrimp were used. Choosing them wasn't hard, Backster noted, since a healthy shrimp appears to spend all its time chasing other shrimp and feverishly practising the propagation of the species.

The model of the experiment was straightforward. The brine shrimp were to be executed by being dumped into boiling water. A randomizing device was used to select one of six time slots when a cup of shrimp was overturned into the simmering bath. The procedure was automated so that no humans were in the laboratory during the experiment.

To serve as controls, drops were made using brine water that contained no shrimp. The point of this, of course, was to see if the plants showed the same tracings as when shrimp were actually dumped into the boiling water.

The experiment is described in detail in the Winter, 1968, issue of the *International Journal of Parapsychology*. The results?

Backster reports that the experiment yielded results five times better than chance would allow.

Other research has followed, and predictably, some of it seems even further out than what has been described.

"We hooked a fertilized but nonincubated egg up to a polygraph," Cleve Backster said. "I got the electrodes attached by placing the egg between two sponges which had been boiled for two or three hours.

"The duration of this run was nine hours. We got the correct heartbeat of a chick embryo of about four days' incubation—157 beats a minute. Yet, when we did an egg embryology and peeled back the shell we found no organism starting to develop to account for this heart action.

"What, then, were we tapping? The blueprint that would have guided this egg to its completion if it had been incubated?

"We found that there was a correlation between the egg and the plants nearby. If a plant leaf was damaged, the polygraph tracing of the egg showed a reaction. Maybe this is what the oneness, the total attunement of all living things, that the mystics speak of is really all about."

The reference to a possible "blueprint" which would have guided the development of the chick embryo if the egg had been incubated has parallels with the research of Burr and Northrup at the Yale Medical School in the 1930s, which indicated that in many species the "morphological pattern" of the embryo was shaped by an electromagnetic field which acted as a kind of mold for the physical body. This field disappeared at the death of the organism.

Cleve Backster's findings also paralleled at many points those of the English scientist, the late George de la Warr; one such point is the notion of "rapport." In de la Warr's thought, rapport refers to a nonphysical link which exists between a subject (human or animal) and his blood-spot or, more significantly in this instance, his photograph. De la Warr maintained that light flashed on a person's photograph correlated with releases of energy into his body, though physically the person might be three thousand miles away. (See de la Warr's book, with Langston Day, *Matter in the Making*, London, Vincent Stuart, 1966.)

"We have found," said Cleve Backster, "that whenever I am away on a speaking engagement, even if it's a thousand miles from New York, the moment the slide of the philodendron that started it all is flashed on the screen, there is a very dramatic reaction by the plant back in the laboratory.

"We've done this many times. I've coordinated it very carefully with my associate who attaches the electrodes to the philodendron. I keep a stopwatch record of the time the picture of the plant is flashed on the screen. At that very instant, back in New York, the polygraph pen takes a leap.

"Distance doesn't seem to affect it. Nor does it appear possible to screen out the signal, whatever it is. We have used complicated shielding but the phenomenon continues. The results have been so consistent that now we're going to structure it into an actual scientific experiment, which could have a lot of profound implications."

De la Warr's theory was that somehow the emulsion on the photograph captures a vital "emanation" from the subject and retains it. An alternative theory is that in Backster's case he was actually in telepathic communication with his associate back in the laboratory and that the plant was detecting the associate's reaction to the signal he received from Backster. However, the phenomenon has occurred even when the associate was out of the laboratory, the plant's polygraph reaction being recorded by an automatic timer on such occasions.

Another possibility is that the plant was in direct telepathic contact with Cleve Backster and was responding to his reaction to the picture being flashed on the screen rather than to the picture itself.

At any rate, telepathy at the very least seems to be involved.

One of the interesting side issues arising from Backster's work is that of how much the expectations and other attitudes of a researcher affect his results. All scientists are aware that they must avoid contaminating the experimental situation by allowing their own prejudices to obtrude. But according to Backster the problem is much deeper and more subtle than that.

"We found," he said,

that if we had anything but the most casual association with the plants before an experiment, they started responding to our moods and reactions and the whole experiment was spoiled.

It is very interesting how the plants tune out, normally, anything that happens outside the walls of the laboratory. We've found that though no physical barrier can screen out the signal that passes from the plant to a human being—and we've tried all kinds of shields—the plant itself can screen out things beyond its immediate environment. It gets tuned in so fantastically on the humans around it that it monitors their moment-by-moment moods.

This is why we had to automate our experiments. The human factor would have altered the results.

This would appear to be true in all biological experiments. A medical researcher, for example, might induce cancer in the experimental animals he's working with by his whole mental involvement in the problem of cancer. There is a lot of re-evaluation which must be done here.

Besides the concept that the thoughts and feelings of researchers modify their experiments to a degree formerly undreamed of, Backster's findings have other, even wider implications.

Think of the impact one person's thought patterns may have on the people around him. On people physically distant from him to whom he is emotionally linked. Or even on people who don't know him.

Consider, too, the impact that the negative thinking of a large number of people could have on others. On a neighborhood. On a city. Or even on a whole nation.

Of all the ramifications of Cleve Backster's work, the possibility of a communications network linking all human beings, and indeed all living things, is the most awesome.

One way of interpreting this is that all living things are parts of a mental substratum; that, as the mystics claim, we are all thoughts in one universal mind.

In this way of looking at things, distance is not geographical—because the mind annihilates space—but psychological. Those with whom we feel at one, we are really close to, even if a thousand miles separates us. And those we are alienated from are distant from us though we share the same room.

I asked Cleve Backster if he thought plants have sensory perception, as humans do. Do they, for example, respond to music?

"No," he said. "Plants respond not to music but to the reactions of the people around them to music.

"We say this because we tried recorded insect noises on the plants. There was no correlation between the noises and the plant responses. Then we put a person in the room and got fantastic correlations. If the person was afraid of a particular insect noise, the plant picked that up.

"We are not dealing with auditory or other sensory perception in plants but something much more profound."

Can plants learn?

"As a matter of fact, we're doing very carefully controlled Pavlovian conditioning experiments with plants," Backster said,

to see if they have memory and if we can teach them things. We've gotten very encouraging results.

You remember how Pavlov did it. He rang a bell and fed the dogs meat. Pretty soon the dogs were salivating at just hearing the bell, even if he didn't give them the meat. They had developed a conditioned response.

We're doing something quite equivalent with plants, only we're using a light deprivation system. We deprive a plant of light for several days and then give it as a reward a twenty-five-second block of time when it's illuminated by a lamp, and then the lamp goes off.

Only upon a certain stimulus does the lamp come on. Then we stop giving the plant the reward but watch for the reaction of *expectancy*. Each time the stimulus associated with the light is presented, we look for the response, though no light actually comes on. It's like Pavlov's dogs salivating at the sound of the bell even when they got no meat.

Our research indicates that memory seems to go down to the cell level in plants. And why not in humans? What's all this fuss about the brain in humans?

The brain is a fantastic switching mechanism but so far as being the exclusive memory-storage device in the human organism—I don't think that's indicated. Total human memory may well be at the cellular level.

This remark bears on the possibility of "genetic memory'" in humans, which is discussed in a later chapter in connection with Ian Stevenson's reincarnation research. Dr. Stevenson's data suggest that some people have memories derived from previous earthly lives. An alternative theory to reincarnation, at least in some cases, is that such people have inherited memories in their genes—just as we inherit our great-grandfather's nose or our great-grandmother's color of eyes.

If memory does indeed function at the cellular level, as Cleve Backster suggests, a vast amount of information could be imprinted on germ plasm and transmitted to subsequent generations. This might explain unlearned behavior among insects—the spider, for example, which spins a complex, highly specialized web without any instruction.

A curious question that Backster raised was the possibility of plant-to-human telepathy as well as vice versa. If plants pick up our messages, do we—unawares, perhaps—pick up theirs?

Many amateur gardeners with a green thumb insist that they talk to their plants, but how many claim that their plants talk back?

And yet, Backster points out, why not? Why shouldn't it be a two-way process?

Anyway, speaking of a green thumb, what is it?

"I think there's a simple explanation," Backster said. "Anybody who sincerely accepts—and the key word is sincerely because you can't just pretend—that there is some kind of sentience or consciousness in plants will have a green thumb. It's a simple as that."

If you love your philodendron, it will love you back?

"Exactly," said Cleve Backster, and he gave the healthy philodendron next to him an affectionate pat.

FIVE

Is There
Psychic Healing?

*If plants respond positively to love and
understanding, and negatively to their op-
posites, what about people? Laboratory
research indicates that there's more than
one way to heal—or to harm. . . .*

FROM TALKING to plants, as Cleve Backster does,
it's only a short step to praying for them. Bernard Grad
took that step.

Dr. Grad, the biologist from McGill University mentioned earlier, doesn't pray for plants himself (unless it's
in private) but he enlists other people to do it in his
laboratory. His purpose: to investigate the so-called
healing force which some people claim flows from their
hands, particularly when they are in a "prayerful" state
of mind.

In a series of experiments (described in full in my
book, *The Unexplained*), Dr. Grad worked with a man
named Oskar Estebany, a retired Hungarian army colonel
now living in Montreal, who declared he had such a healing power. In the experiments, twenty-four peat pots were
filled with soil and twenty barley seeds planted in each.
The pots were randomly divided into two equal groups.
Dr. Grad asked Mr. Estebany to hold in his hands a bottle
of saline solution (water with 1 percent salt added)
and try to infuse it with his healing force. This solution
was then poured over the experimental plants, the plants
in the control group receiving only "untreated" (not
prayed over or handled) saline solution.

The experiment lasted fourteen days. The results? The
plants which received the "treated" solution grew significantly taller and more robust than those in the other
group.

Grad concluded that there is a force, linked to a
prayerful mental state (Mr. Estebany said he was in such

57

a mood when he generated his healing energy), which can stimulate cell growth in plants. Further experiments indicated that Mr. Estebany's power also speeded up the healing of surgical wounds in laboratory mice.

Certain questions occurred to Bernard Grad: Was there a negative as well as a positive polarity to this healing force? Could growth or healing be inhibited by somebody in a, so to speak, antiprayerful state of mind?

To get some answers, he set up a particularly intriguing experiment. It involved three subjects: a normal person, a fifty-two-year-old male identified as J. B.; a twenty-six-year-old woman under psychiatric treatment for neurotic depression, identified as R. H.; and a thirty-seven-year-old male psychiatric patient with an acute psychotic depression, identified as H. R.

The hypothesis which the experiment was designed to test: A saline solution held for thirty minutes in the hands of a normal individual in a happy, confident state of mind would induce plants watered with it to grow better than would identical solutions similarly held by depressed people.

To round out the experiment a control bottle of saline solution was introduced which would receive no handling from anyone.

The experiment procedure was simple. Each person in turn held a sealed bottle of sterile saline solution (such as is normally used for intravenous infusions in humans) between his or her hands for thirty minutes, then poured the solution on barley seeds embedded in soil. The control solution, which was not "treated" by anyone, also was poured over planted barley seeds.

Other conditions of the experiment were standardized. All the barley seeds came from the same source; the soil was identical in each case; and all seeds received the same amounts of sunlight and tap water.

The term of the experiment was sixteen days. Daily measurements of the seedlings were made as soon as they appeared above the soil. At the termination of the experiment, the seedlings were measured root and shoot.

The results?

The plants "treated" by the normal person grew better, and there were more of them, than the others. The neurotic's plants grew second best, the control plants were next down the scale, and those of the psychotic subject grew least. The differences in growth were statistically significant.

At first it appeared that the results did not fully confirm Dr. Grad's hypothesis. True, the plants of the depressed individuals grew less than those of the normal person. But those of the neurotic woman did better than the control group—the seedlings which received the "untreated" saline solution—and markedly better than those of the psychotic depressive. Why these variances?

It was in probing this question that Grad defined more clearly how the hypothetical healing force operated.

He zeroed in on the emotional state of each person at the time he or she was holding the saline solution, prior to pouring it over the seeds. The normal subject, J. B., said that during his "treatment" of the solution he was in the same state of mind as when he prayed for the recovery of a sick member of his family. He described it as a mood in which he tried to sense "something" flowing through his hands and into the solution in the bottle. He willed that the solution would trap the "something" and hold it.

The neurotic depressive, R. H., whose plants came second to J. B.'s in growth, appeared to be morose until she was told the purpose of the experiment. She reacted with pleased surprise and a noticeable brightening of mood, Grad recalled. During the thirty-minute period she cradled the bottle in her lap, like a mother holding a child.

By contrast, H. R., the psychotic depressive, was agitated, anxious, and melancholy when he came into the experiment room, and he appeared to become even more so as the "treatment" proceeded. During the time he was holding the bottle he expressed no interest in the purpose of the experiment, only in how quickly he would be able to leave the mental hospital.

Dr. Grad observed that there appeared to be a correlation between the mood of each subject as he held his saline solution and the growth of the particular barley seeds over which the solution was poured. He had expected both depressed subjects to inhibit growth of their plants; however his mistake, he reasoned, was in considering only their long-term psychiatric condition and not making allowance for mood changes. Taking that into consideration, the experimental results were precisely what had been expected—the normal subject's plants grew best;

59

those of the neurotic depressive, whose mood brightened during the experiment, next best; the "control" ones next; and those of the psychotic depressive, who remained negative-minded during the experiment, grew least of all.

Grad's finding that the mood-of-the-moment is most important in the healing (or antihealing) situation was corroborated, he remembered, by some preliminary tests he had done with two psychiatric patients who were able to stimulate yeast cell activity by holding a bottle of the culture. These patients, though under treatment for melancholia, were amused at the thought of being asked to hold a bottle and entered into the experiment with rare (for them) enthusiasm.

Certain conclusions appeared to follow from this experiment.

1. A positive mood while holding saline solution produces or makes possible a change in the solution which leads to a relative stimulation of cell growth in plants watered with the solution.
2. A negative mood, such as depression, anxiety, or hostility, while holding such a solution results in an inhibition of cell growth in plants watered with the solution.
3. The plus or minus growth factor can be transmitted with only one initial treatment.

It seemed that whatever the growth or antigrowth factor was, it impregnated the saline solution. It could not be a chemical, such as in sweat or breath, because it passed through the sealed glass jars containing the solution. Therefore it must be an energy. And it appeared to be generated by a strong emotional reaction.

Needless to say, mainstream science knows nothing at present of such an energy—one with a dual aspect (positive or negative), engendered by human emotional states, and capable of charging a medium (the saline solution).

However, Soviet scientists are doing a lot of research in what they call "bioenergetic radiation," which bears many similarities to the X-force investigated by Bernard Grad.

The Soviet story began more than forty years ago when biologist Alexander Gurvich—with whose work Grad is familiar—discovered a force he dubbed mitogenetic radiation. He said it appeared when plant cells divide (a process known as mitosis).

In the 1960s, other Soviet scientists rediscovered Gurvich's work. Dr. Vlail Kaznacheyev established, to his own satisfaction at least, that very weak radiations are involved in cell division. He also found that sick cells could make healthy cells diseased without having actual contact with them if this mysterious "mitogenetic radiation" passed from one to the other. This suggested that sickness may be catching in a subtle way no one had yet imagined.

Two Soviet physicians, Dr. Lyudmila Kulikova and Dr. Mikhail Nabiulin, independently discovered that weak radiation of some unidentified sort is emitted by human blood, and this radiation changes markedly, and characteristically, when people fall ill.

Shiela Ostrander and Lynn Schroeder, two perceptive young ladies who are also connoisseurs of psychical research in the Eastern European countries, told me that the most provocative work they observed in a recent tour of the Soviet Union was that of Sergei Kirlian and his wife, discoverers of the "Kirlian Effect." This pertains to an unusual form of photography devised by the Kirlians which makes visible a fantastically dazzling "aura" or color spectrum around living things. More important, the aura changes when the organism is sick.

A healthy leaf photographed by the Kirlians in a high-frequency radiation field revealed a cosmos of unimaginable beauty, alive with twinkles, flashes, sparkles, shooting flares, and miniature soaring comets in colors of gold, red, blue, and violet, all intermingling. When the leaf was torn from the plant, the aura diminished and after a few hours disappeared.

The Kirlians discovered that their method of photography revealed radiation streaming from the hands of some self-styled healers. One man, called only Krivorotov by the Kirlians, was found to give off spectacular streams of energy from his fingertips when he put himself in a healing mood.

Also, the Kirlians reported that they were able to photograph changes in the auras of other people some of them ill, when Krivorotov laid hands on them. It was as though the radiation from his hands reorganized or recharged the sick people's auras.

The exact nature of these healing radiations is considered unknown by the Soviet scientists. But may incline strongly to the view that they are a form of electromagnetism. Some refer to the force as "biomagnetism," literally, magnetism emitted by a living organism. There is parallel research in the United States and Canada to which I will refer shortly.

However, to return to Dr. Bernard Grad: He points out more characteristics of the X-force which can either heal or harm.

The healing process, he suggests, is an equation involving the healer and the one-to-be-healed and the attitudes of both are important. On the healer's side there usually is a state of mind which, whether explicitly religious or not, certainly could be called devotional, or perhaps inspirational. And on the side of the patient, a certain attitude of acceptance is desirable.

"Persons who claim to have the gift of healing have often stated that the work of healing is not done by them but by some Higher Power with whom the healer claims to be in contact," said Dr. Grad. "This he does through evoking some positive emotion in himself, such as submission to the will of God or the affirmation that 'Jesus heals,' etc.

"Also, such persons claim that for best results, the sufferer should also be accepting in the sense that he should be in a positive emotional state or, at the very least, not in a negative one, while the healing is being attempted. . . ."

Grad referred to a parallel situation in the experiment on wound-healing in mice. It was found that "significant accelerations of the wound-healing process occurred only in mice that were made calm and accepting by stroking their fur gently for short periods . . . before the experiment began." Mice that were nervous and agitated during the time the healer laid hands on them (actually, held them between his hands) failed to respond to the treatment.

It would appear, then, that negative emotions in the creature receiving the laying on of hands creates a barrier which the healing force does not penetrate.

Grad points out that even in orthodox medicine, psychotherapy particularly, the prognosis of patients who do not voluntarily seek treatment is poor. The patient-against-his-will probably won't respond to anything, from tender loving care to the latest wonder drug.

Reference has been made to Soviet experiments which suggest that the healing force is electromagnetic in nature —that is, it belongs to the electromagnetic spectrum and probably takes the form of therapeutic "waves" which presumably would be detectable by appropriate instruments. Some research sparked by Dr. Grad's work appears to offer support for this electromagnetic theory.

A Roman Catholic nun with a Ph.D. in biochemistry has gotten her own laboratory evidence of the phenomenon of "healing hands." Sister M. Justa Smith, chairman of the chemistry department at Rosary Hill College, Buffalo, told me about her off-the-beaten-track research.

She started it, she said, after studying Dr. Grad's work with Mr. Estebany, the man who stimulated plant growth. Sister Justa came up with a hypothesis of her own in connection with the laying-on-of-hands syndrome. Her theory derived from the fact that all the metabolic reactions of every body cell are regulated by specific biochemicals called enzymes. So important are these enzymes that they are often called the "brains" of the cells.

It would seem to follow, or so Sister Justa felt, that any disease proceeds from some aberration of enzyme activity—a lack, or a malfunctioning. And any change from sickness to health would require a prior change in the catalysts—the enzymes.

Sister Justa's hypothesis then was: "Any healing force channeled through or activated by the hands or presence of an unorthodox healer must affect enzyme activity if healing is to take place." To test the hypothesis she conducted a series of experiments with Mr. Estebany, the man with the healing hands.

The model of the experiment was straightforward. Choosing a common enzyme called trypsin, Sister Justa proposed to observed and compare any effects from Estebany's hands with those produced by ultraviolet light and high magnetic fields. It was known that ultraviolet light reduced the enzyme's activity by 60 to 80 percent; Sister Justa wanted to find out if Mr. Estebany could revitalize this sick enzyme. The influence of a magnetic field* was more ambiguous, but Sister Justa wished to determine if the magnetic radiation had the same effect on the enzyme as the force from Mr. Estebany's hands.

Every day, during the period of the experiment, four bottles of trypsin solution were prepared. The first—the control—received no treatment. The second was held in Estebany's hands for seventy-five minutes. The third was

---

* A magnetic field is a field of influence generated by an electric current passing between a negative and positive pole

first irradiated with ultraviolet and then held by Estebany. The fourth solution was exposed to a strong magnetic field for periods up to four hours.

"The results," said Sister Justa, "indicated greatly increased activity of the treated enzymes over the control solution."

The accelerated activity of the enzyme in the bottle held by the healer was comparable to that obtained in the strong magnetic field. Also, the rate of activity in the enzymes that had been damaged or inhibited by the ultraviolet radiation returned to normal levels after being held by him.

"It is interesting," said Sister Justa, "that the qualitative effect of a high magnetic field and of the hands of this man are the same. They are also quantitatively similar."

In other words, enzyme activity increased both after treatment by Mr. Estebany and after magnetism, and the rate of increase was almost identical.

This last detail could be interpreted to mean that the healing force emitted by Mr. Estebany is a form of biomagnetism. This is possible, but it would be premature to draw that conclusion from Sister Justa's research. Similar consequences can follow from totally dissimilar causes: a man may be rendered unconscious by a blow on the head, a drug, hypnosis, a circulatory disorder, or a sudden emotional shock, to name just a few possible agents.

A definitive test—at any rate, as definitive as today's science could make it—of whether the healing force is physical or nonphysical (i.e., part of the electromagnetic spectrum or outside it) would be whether it penetrates lead shielding or other barriers known to screen out physical radiations. Dr. Grad told me that his research ended before he could apply such tests. But his guess, he confessed with a knowing smile, was that the X-force goes through lead and other barriers as a jet of flame would go through a spider's web.

He referred to certain Soviet experiments which suggested a nonphysical nature to psychic forces (a category to which he implied the healing energy belongs). He mentioned that the late Russian parapsychologist, Dr. L. L. Vasiliev, reported an experiment with telepathic hypnosis in which the subject was enclosed in a lead-lined cabinet which was then immersed in a mercury bath—a double barrier. Yet the subject apparently received the telepathic transmission, dutifully going into a deep hypnotic trance at a mental suggestion from the hypnotist.

(Without getting unduly technical, it is pertinent to point out here that the line between "physical" and "non-physical" is becoming more and more blurred as physics probes deeper into reality and edges closer and closer to the realm of what might be called psychics—the shadowy area where mind and matter meet. Suffice it to say that the neutrino, a subatomic particle, apparently glides through several feet of lead as though it weren't there and yet it presumably belongs, in the broadest sense, to the world of physical energy.)

The question arises: If human beings can generate an unknown force by emotional actions, capable of either stimulating or retarding (or even regressing) growth, depending on the type of emotion, what are the limits of this power's capability?

Are there unusually gifted people who may possess this power to such a degree, for one reason or another, that they can produce "miracles"?

My book, *Kathryn Kuhlman: The Woman Who Believes in Miracles,* documents such a person, a Pittsburgh-based evangelist who is the greatest charismatic healer of our time. In Kathryn Kuhlman's services, under the enchantment of her personality, tumors regress, cataracts melt from eyes, broken or deformed bones straighten, deaf ears become unstopped, dead nerves are regenerated, and destroyed tissue is restored. All these phenomena are documented in my book with the names of those healed and of the doctors who attest to the healings.

When one faces the question of whether this healing force has *any* limitations—well, it's exceedingly difficult to say. Certain things spring to mind as being about as impossible as anybody could imagine—a missing limb being re-created, for example, or a glass eye turning into a real one. But what about teeth being filled by psychic means? This is exactly what is claimed by the most curious of all present-day, self-styled faith healers—the Reverend Willard Fuller. He is the nephew of the late Reverend Charles E. Fuller, director of what was once the most widely broadcast religious radio program in the world, "The Old-Fashioned Revival Hour."

"Does God fill teeth?" asked the religious tract that came into my office at the *Toronto Daily Star.* It was an invitation to a divine healing mission conducted by the Louisiana-born evangelist, who purports to practise a sort of transcendental dentistry.

This was in February, 1969; the evangelist was scheduled to pray for bad teeth at the United Apostolic Faith Church, an offshoot Pentecostal congregation in the Toronto suburb of Scarborough.

My curiosity unwound itself and began stretching. I had heard reports from here and there about Mr. Fuller's unusual ministry; my impression was that he was a rather elusive individual whose meetings were advertised mainly by word of mouth among the faithful. This was to be my first chance to see him in action.

He was already very much in action when I arrived at the service to join the two hundred or so in attendance.

"God puts gold, silver, or porcelain fillings in cavities," he exclaimed. "I don't know why some people get gold or silver and others porcelain but"—and he shrugged—"there are many things about this God-given ministry I don't understand."

The fiftyish, wavy-haired revivalist mopped his brow and smiled broadly, his pearly teeth gleaming. (Later he allowed that they were false.)

"If God can put silver or gold in a mountain, He can put it in your mouth!" he roared, thumping the pulpit.

"God'll heal you through this ministry of anything that's wrong with your mouth. That includes cavities, gingivitis, receding gums, gum boils, malocclusion, teeth that need to be straightened, or a lack of teeth from one to thirty-two.

"I haven't got perfect faith for heart trouble or eye trouble or cancer," he declared, his voice rising in volume, "but one thing I know—God heals teeth!"

The last three words were thunderclaps.

Before inviting those with missing molars and other dental defects to come forward for prayer, the evangelist hammered home some more faith-building precepts.

"You walk in the atmosphere of your own believing," he shouted,

and my belief is that God heals teeth.

One night while I was holding services in Michigan a visiting pastor told me, with great excitement, that one of the ladies of his church was walking in the business section of town about noon that day and thinking about how she wished she could attend the services. She hadn't been able to attend because she worked at night. She had a cavity that was so bad the dentist couldn't do anything for it.

Then, the pastor said, the lady felt a peculiar sensation in the tooth that had the cavity. She remembered that her friends said they felt sensations in their teeth when their cavities were filled. She was in front of the Kress Store and she went inside and looked into a mirror. She found that the cavity was filled with beautiful silver.

'Tell me, Brother Fuller,' the pastor asked, 'how did she get her healing?'

I told him to phone the lady and ask her, without prompting, whether the healing happened at about 9:45 that morning. He came back after phoning her and said, yes, it was about quarter till ten when the tooth was filled. He asked how I knew that was the time.

Because, my brother, I told him, this morning at 9:45 I walked in front of the Kress Store. And we walk in the atmosphere of our own believing. Others may say whatever they please, but one thing I know: God will fill teeth! I walk in that belief. I walk in the belief that the gifts of the Spirit are real. I believe that God manifests Himself through signs and wonders.

Then the evangelist invited those who wanted prayer for dental blessings to come forward. About fifty people lined up across the front of the sanctuary. Willard Fuller, armed with a dental mirror and a bottle of fluid, passed down the row. (Later he told me the fluid was an antiseptic used to sterilize the dental mirror—purely, he added, to avoid conflict with health laws since "if God can fill teeth He can certainly take care of germs.")

The evangelist appeared to choose people at random, or as though he were obeying some inner prompting. Some people he passed over the first time, then backtracked to pray for them. He was accompanied by the church pastor, the Reverend Maxwell Whyte, who watched everything intently.

Peering into a middle-aged man's mouth with the mirror, Fuller said: "He's got two small cavities. There and there."

Whyte peered in and nodded.

Fuller placed his hands on both sides of the man's jaw and expostulated: "Lord, heal these teeth! For Jesus' sake!"

It sounded more like a command, or at least an urgent recommendation, than a petition.

Peering again into the man's mouth, the evangelist broke into a wide grin.

"Look now," he invited.

The pastor, Mr. Whyte, stuck his head close to the man's mouth, squinted, and murmured something. Then he turned to the congregation and announced: "Brother Fuller's absolutely right. This brother here has two gold fillings that weren't there a moment ago."

The congregation exploded into cries of "Hallelujah!" "Glory to God!" and "Thank you, Jesus!"

The man for whom Fuller had just prayed told me later that he was Hugo Mittendorf from Sharon, Ontario, a small town about twenty-five miles from Toronto. He said that he had not been aware of the two cavities the evangelist reported spotting.

"But I do know I didn't have gold fillings," he added, "and look for yourself."

Two large fillings that looked like gold gleamed at me from a pair of lower molars.

Mr. Mittendorf, a member of the Pentecostal church in Newmarket, Ontario, said he believed in miracles and really wasn't too surprised by the fillings.

Others at the service professed to have experienced unusual dental phenomena. Mrs. Ann Carter of Toronto informed me that she had instantly gotten a gold filling where there had been none. Mrs. Arthur Pressey of Scarborough said her teeth "started to gleam, after Brother Fuller prayed for me, as they had never gleamed before." Her teeth, I had to admit, were as white as those in any television commercial.

Mrs. Maxwell Whyte, the pastor's wife, who struck me as a sensible person, pointed out two small white spots on each of two of her teeth. The evangelist said that these were new enamel, in the process of forming, to protect areas where the natural covering had worn thin. According to him, the spots probably would increase considerably in size. However, three months later when I checked back they were still the same size—barely larger in circumference, say, than ten pinheads combined. Her own

68

dentist had examined them, Mrs. Whyte reported, and agreed that they looked like enamel, although no tests were made. The dentist apparently offered no explanation for them.

Others in the church claimed to have had crooked teeth straightened—some instantly, some gradually. One man told me that during the healing service what felt like a new tooth started to push up through his gum. Three months later, Mr. Whyte reported that the man claimed to have a normal tooth, but I wasn't able to interview him myself.

Willard Fuller was ordained a Southern Baptist minister (this is the denomination to which Billy Graham belongs) and has degrees in business administration, mechanical engineering, and theology, the latter from New Orleans Southern Baptist Theological Seminary. He left the Southern Baptist Convention in 1960.

When did his healing ministry start? And, I asked him, why *teeth?*

"I know it sounds pretty strange," he confessed with a wry half-smile.

"If I had my choice I suppose I wouldn't have picked teeth to heal. Probably anything else. But there you are. Many things about this ministry I don't understand."

Born in Grant Parish, Louisiana, in 1915, Willard Fuller experienced a religious conversion when he was fourteen, and felt the "call to preach" when he was seventeen. After his return from military service in World War Two, he enrolled in a seminary. For more than ten years he was a conventional clergyman, pastoring a succession of four Southern Baptist congregations.

Then, in 1960, he had the cataclysmic experience which Pentecostals call "the baptism of the Holy Spirit." He was transported in ecstasy, and burst forth in the rhapsodic utterance known as "speaking in tongues," which the skeptic dismisses as gibberish, but which the true believer interprets as a heavenly language.

Three days later, something even more spectacular happened.

"God spoke to me in an audible voice," Fuller told me. He paused, his eyes searching my face.

"Yes, an *audible* voice. The Lord said, 'Son, I've given you the gift of healing miracles.' "

After this experience, noted Fuller, people were healed

in his services of such ailments as stomach ulcers, arthritis, asthma, and warts.

In March, 1960, came the strangest experience of all. Willard Fuller attended a service conducted by an evangelist named A. C. McKaig who was said to have the gift of supernaturally filling teeth. During the service McKaig prayed that Fuller too might receive this gift.

Laying his hands on Fuller's head, the other evangelist appeared to fall under a mystic thrall. He spoke in oracular tones: "Think it not strange, My son, that I do these things through My servant, for all the things that thou hast seen Me do through him I shall do through thee, and greater things. . . ."

Then, apparently coming to himself, the evangelist prayed in more normal, though fervent, tones: "Now, Lord, give him a double portion of Thy power."

At that moment, says Willard Fuller, he felt an electric shock. The room began to recede and then rush back to him. He slid to the floor in a trancelike state. (Pentecostals call this "going down under the power." It is also a feature of the ministry of Kathryn Kuhlman.)

"From then on," said Fuller, "people started getting their teeth filled in my meetings."

Asked why God would fill teeth with gold, silver, and porcelain and not create new natural enamel, the evangelist shrugged.

"I don't know. I stopped a long time ago trying to figure out why God does things. But take a small child, ten or twelve years of age, who's never been to the dentist in her life. Then God fills her cavities with silver or gold. When someone else sees these fillings and knows the child has never been to a dentist, it is going to make an impact. But if the teeth were all restored to wholeness, there would always be some doubt as to whether there had ever been anything wrong with them in the first place."

Some critics, not too surprisingly, have suggested that the evangelist may give God a helping hand with the fillings. George Bishop, a Los Angeles writer, reported that a woman, whom he doesn't name, received a grayish filling in a Willard Fuller service. A dentist, Dr. Edwin M. Gordon, reportedly examined it and described it as a common, inexpensive cement used by most dentists as a temporary filling. X-rays were taken, according to Bishop, which revealed advanced decay under the temporary filling. The dentist urged immediate removal of the filling, and treatment, to avoid losing the tooth.

Bishop speculated on how the filling might have arrived in the tooth.

"Yes," the dentist replied to a question, "the filling could be held on the ball of the thumb and simply pressed into the cavity. This could be done with a natural motion that would probably leave the patient unaware that anything had happened."

It would be quite feasible, Bishop suggested, for the cement filling to be stuck to the underside of a dental mirror and pressed into the cavity from there. The dentist agreed.

In a book about Willard Fuller, *Can God Fill Teeth?* (Lakemont, Georgia, CSA Press, 1970), author Daniel Fry deals with this reported incident. He claims that there are instances in which a temporary filling, such as the woman in Bishop's story received, has been spontaneously replaced by a permanent substance, through Fuller's ministry.

According to author Fry, a woman got a filling that looked "gummy, like putty." The next day she picked the substance out of the cavity. It was similar in appearance to the material many dentists use for temporary fillings. Ashamed of what she had done through curiosity, the woman, says Fry, prayed earnestly that God would forgive her and complete the healing.

"The cavity filled up again with the same substance," he writes, "that looked like a temporary filling. About one week later this changed to a porcelain-type material and remained in that state."

In May, 1968, Aldon Taft, religion editor of Florida's *Miami Herald* wrote a report on Willard Fuller who was then conducting services in that city.

Fillings turning to gold, cavities being filled, and teeth being straightened are among some of the dental "healings" being reported in a series of unusual meetings in progress at the Evangel Temple, 3516 N.W. Seventh Ave.

"I've never seen anything like this," declared the Reverend Martin Luther Davidson, pastor of the Assemblies of God church. One of the leading ministers in a denomination in which healing services are a regular practice, the Reverend Mr. Davidson is

71

known to be very cautious and slow to endorse the work of any of the so-called faith healers. Oral Roberts is one of only three whose ministries he supports.

"But I've never before seen dental healings," he said. "And these things happened right before our eyes."

He referred to the events which took place Tuesday night in a service conducted by the Reverend Willard Fuller, of Mountain View, California.

"I have a cavity in the process of being filled," insisted Mrs. Evelyn Marzullo, 1794 S.W. 19th St., who pointed to a tooth which appeared to have a large white filling except for a small black spot in the middle. She said the whole top of the tooth had been black when "threads of white began circling the cavity and began filling it" during the Tuesday night service.

A Catholic, who had come to the service with a friend, Mrs. Marzullo said that a filling in another tooth had turned to gold when she joined a line of about one hundred people upon whom the Rev. Mr. Fuller laid his hands and prayed.

About half of those reported some sort of dental healing, according to the Rev. Mr. Davidson. But some of them actually were not healed, noted the Rev. Mr. Fuller.

"There are always a few people who become emotional and think something happened that did not," he said. "One woman thought her fillings had turned to gold and went to her dentist to tell him what had happened to her. He reminded her that he had put in the gold fillings himself some time ago."

On the other hand, there are those like Mrs. Ann Mitchell, 1942 Taylor St., Hollywood, who displayed a gold tooth at the very back of her upper jaw which she said was not gold before.

In fact, she added, it was almost entirely black from decay that two years ago prompted her to consider having it pulled. But since that tooth was anchoring a bridge which covered most of her upper jaw, the decision was to keep it as long as possible.

A check with the Fort Lauderdale dentist who has

treated Mrs. Mitchell for twelve years confirmed at least that he did not gold plate the tooth.

Mrs. Cynthia Reddy, 14500 Mahogany Ct., Miami Lakes, who said her teeth had been discolored all her life, smiled to show a row of white teeth she said got that way during the service.

The teeth were not quite straight but she said they were much better than ever before, when they overlapped. "I can run my tongue along them without it catching now," she said.

During the service, Mrs. Reddy recalled, "it felt like my jaw was being stretched."

The Rev. Mr. Fuller has letters in which people testify that a new tooth has instantaneously grown into a space where a permanent tooth had been knocked out or pulled. Names and addresses of dentists are included. . . .

"I don't know what happens or how God does it," said the Rev. Mr. Fuller. "All I know is that it happens."

It has not happened to him or his wife, both of whom have dental deficiencies.

He said it happened to more than one-thousand persons a year since he "received the baptism of the Holy Spirit. . . ."

Another press report about Fuller, dated June 22, 1967, appeared in the *Valley Advertiser-Herald Tribune,* in Southern California:

"Supernatural tooth fillings that didn't look like any metal I've ever seen before," were described to the *Valley Times* today by a Chatsworth dentist.

Preferring not to use his name, the dentist said the patient with the fillings told him that the dental work had been done immediately after a Valley faith healer prayed for her.

Describing himself as a member of the Valley Dental Society and the American Dental Association, the dentist said he had several patients with extra teeth and several with fillings that had been done, they said, "by a supernatural force."

"The fillings are lighter than gold and yet more yellow than silver," he said. "I've attended conferences of dentists and have never seen anything like this before."

The patient whose filled teeth are intriguing is Frieda Tauriello, who says she experienced the faith healing at Canna Miracle Tabernacle in Sylmar.

Daniel Fry's book about Willard Fuller bristles with testimonies. Some of them are curious in the extreme. This unusual ministry has even stranger features than at first appear.

Mrs. O. Ruddick of Pueblo, Colorado, avers that in a Fuller service, "I saw a cavity on a five-year-old boy being filled with a white material moving with a slow, circular motion. I kept saying to myself, 'What am I seeing?' I was on the borderline of doubt. . . ."

Mrs. Ruddick goes on to say that she took a nine-year-old deaf boy with two large dental cavities to the next service. Nothing happened during the service, but it did later at home.

"It was 11:10 P.M.," states Mrs. Ruddick's account. "Myself, and his mother and father, looked into the little deaf boy's mouth. His teeth were being filled slowly with a circular movement and a white material was being molded into the cavity as we watched. I was so excited I was speechless. My God! It's happening. . . . The name of the little deaf child is Bobbie Reiss."

Some people testify that teeth with fillings in them were replaced by whole natural teeth through Willard Fuller:

"I, Paul Richard Bailey of San Diego, California, on the night of July 28, 1965, at the Revival Assembly, San Diego, received two silver fillings in my mouth where I had two cavities. Also, three old composition fillings that the dentist had put in many years ago disappeared completely, leaving perfect whole teeth."

Some people claim to have received several fillings, of different substances.

Vivian Williams of Louisville, Kentucky, said: "God wonderfully filled two of my teeth after Brother Fuller prayed. One filling is of porcelain and the other silver."

Daniel Fry claims that occasionally new materials show up. One cavity was filled with a rubylike substance, he insists; another, with bronze; another, with a platinumlike metal; and still another, with a substance that sparkled like diamonds.

Sometimes the evangelist adds practicality to faith by

telling people with gum diseases to go home and brush their gums twice a day for seven days and they will be healed. Their "obedience and faith" contribute to the healing, he suggests.

In addition to healing, Willard Fuller claims to have the gift of what he calls "knowing," or, as a parapsychologist would label it, clairvoyance. Sometimes, he says, he can tell what's wrong with a person's mouth before he looks into it. And sometimes he divines personal secrets in an individual's life. His choice of whom he prays for is made on the basis of this inner "knowing."

Other peculiar phenomena are reported. Fireballs are said to have hovered over churches where Willard Fuller was ministering. Some people profess to have seen lights playing around his head.

One of the most curious incidents of all is cited in a letter, whose writer is unnamed: "One woman in the service just wouldn't believe God could do these things. Gerald and I and a few others, strangers to us, watched a decayed tooth of this woman's turn gold, back to decay, back to gold, back to decay—three times. You might find this hard to believe but it happened before our eyes. That woman left with the decay although the gold seemed to have tried to stay there. For the first time in our lives we had some understanding of the words of Jesus when He said, 'Let it be according to your faith.'"

In my conversation with Willard Fuller, I asked him whether he himself could detect any pattern in the bizarre stories told—why one person got gold fillings, another silver, and another porcelain or some exotic substance like ruby or diamond? Why was one healed instantly and another gradually? Or why did one person get a filling on-the-spot, while another received it several hours, days, or even weeks later?

"The answer," Fuller said, "is that today I find no pattern to this."

After Willard Fuller had left Toronto, I asked Maxwell Whyte, who had been his host pastor, for his impressions of Fuller's ministry.

The pastor told me that there were aspects of Mr. Fuller's ministry which he did not like ("his gypsylike style of living and the way he took up a love offering for himself"), but he personally had no doubts about the genuineness of the dental healings.

"It's true," said Mr. Whyte, "that some people thought

75

they had new fillings and then found out from their dentist that they'd had them all along. But others did have results that can't be explained—unless they're just absolutely deluded.

"My wife has the two little white spots on her teeth that have persisted for weeks and the dentist can't explain them. My daughter-in-law's old fillings gleam as if they had been refurbished and the dentist can't explain that. Nobody in our church has had a filling fall out. One man says he has a whole new tooth, a natural one that wasn't there before.

"As for any suggestion of Mr. Fuller sticking the fillings in—I totally reject that. Thirty fillings in one night?"

What do I think of Willard Fuller's phenomena?

Well, they are far out, of course. The question is whether they are far out enough—as atomic physicist Niels Bohr put it—to be true.

For the psychical researcher there are some provocative features of Fuller's ministry: His apparent clairvoyant ability which works as an adjunct to his purported healing gift; and the luminescent effects ("auric" manifestations?) some people report in his presence. The accounts of miniature white tornadoes, fantastic as they seem, to some researchers may suggest ectoplasm—the mysterious malleable-by-mind substance said to be drawn from the bodies of some mediums.

One noted clairvoyant, with whom I discussed Willard Fuller's idiosyncratic ministry, speculated that, assuming the healings to be genuine, the tooth fillings may be apports—objects or substances inexplicably transported from one place to another by psychic means. In this case, Willard Fuller would be a "physical" medium without knowing it. (Or maybe he does know it; there are hints in his statements that he inclines toward a psychic interpretation of the phenomena.)

Spiritualists might go on to theorize that the reason why he specializes in teeth healing is that his "spirit guide" is a discarnate dentist who's taken up the astral equivalent of his old profession!

My feeling is that the phenomenon of transcendental dentistry is prima facie enticing enough to merit further investigation. With proper methods, it shouldn't be too hard to determine whether Willard Fuller is indeed the most curious psychic healer around, or something else. . . .

Bernard Grad's research, indicating that the X-force can harm or hinder, depending on the emotional state of the person generating it, led me to an experiment with an adult education class in parapsychology that I was teaching at Ryerson Polytechnical Institute, Toronto. This had some intriguing results.

I made no scientific claims for the experiment. However, E. Douglas Dean, former president of the Parapsychological Association, was very interested when I described it to him and said he would try it himself. Later he reported significant results and said he planned further similar experiments.

The experiment was designed to test the notion that people can generate a force which, on the one hand, stimulates growth and, on the other, hinders it. We formulated our hypothesis this way: If identical seeds receive more or less identical treatment and, in addition, one group is "blessed" and the other "blighted," the first will grow significantly more and the second significantly less than a control group.

We decided to use barley seeds for the experiment, for the reasons cited by Dr. Grad: They grow quickly, and they grow straight up, which makes the seedlings easy to measure.

We had to standardize the conditions of the experiment. To do this perfectly we would have needed a climatorium or growth chamber in which such factors as moisture, humidity, and temperature could be kept uniform for all the seeds. For practical reasons this wasn't possible. So, realizing that we had less than a scientifically ideal situation, we tried to standardize as much as possible.

All barley seeds used in the experiment came from the same bag purchased at a Toronto garden supply house. The soil similarly came from the same bag. A uniform amount of soil was put into identical peat pots.

Before describing the treatment the seeds were to receive, let me discuss how we divided the experimenters into "blessers," "blighters," and "controls."

To understand the rationale of my choice it is necessary to consider some features of extrasensory perception discovered by Dr. J. B. Rhine and his associates during their groundbreaking research thirty years ago at the former Duke University parapsychology laboratory. To test for ESP (Rhine invented the term), he employed card-guessing, using what are called Zener cards (after the psychologist who designed them) or ESP cards. These consist of a pack of twenty-five cards of five kinds bearing, respectively, the following symbols: a cross, circle, star, rectangle, and wavy lines.

Various tests were designed for different forms of psychic perception. For telepathy (mind-to-mind contact) a receiver tried to guess the order in which cards were turned up by a sender (both the sender, and the cards, being hidden behind a screen, or sometimes in another room). For clairvoyance (mind-to-object contact) the receiver tried to guess the sequence of cards turned up, but not looked at, by the sender. For precognition (mind-to-future-event contact) the receiver tried to guess in what order the cards would be shuffled by machinery at some future date.

Central to the experiments was what mathematicians call the probability theory—the laws of chance. To illustrate: Consider the tossing of a coin. Let's say that we're trying to come up with heads; therefore, getting heads is a hit and tails a miss. The probability theory says that if you come up with heads seven times in a row, the odds against that being due to chance are 128 to 1. And they increase astronomically thereafter. When you get up to odds of a 1,000 to 1, you can be sure something besides chance is at work.

Applying probability factors to card-guessing, the chance level of hits on four runs through the ESP pack—a hundred cards—is 20, one card in five. If you get 28 hits, the odds against chance are 20 to 1, or fair. If you get 32, the odds against chance jump to 250 to 1. Those are excellent results. Of course, to be really significant, such results would have to be sustained over more than one run.

Now—and this is important in terms of the experiment I designed—if you score below chance—say 12 instead of 20 out of a hundred—that is also statistically significant. And Rhine had subjects who did this. He called the phenomenon "psi-missing." The theory is that the subjects unconsciously tried to avoid the target. These misses were really disguised hits, or negative hits, if you like, and, if consistent, were just as strong evidence for antichance as the positive hits. They seemed to indicate a sort of reverse ESP.

It occurred to me that the phenomenon of psi-missing

might well be related to the growth inhibition effect. Both seemed to be an inversion. Would people who proved to be psi-missers on card-guessing also prove to be powerful inhibitors of growth? It was worth finding out.

There were only thirty in my parapsychology class, too small a group to get really significant results. But then, the experiment, as I had explained to the class from the first, was a tentative, preliminary probe; its results at best could be considered only suggestive.

The class took part in a card-guessing session in which I went through the ESP pack four times—the minimum run to get any meaningful results—looking at each card for thirty seconds, then turning it face down on the desk in front of me. The cards were hidden from the class by an opaque screen. Between each run, the pack was shuffled.

On the basis of their scores the class members were divided into three groups: Those who scored above chance were the "blessers," those below were the "blighters" and those at or near the chance level formed the control group. We came up with three groups of ten each.

The barley seeds were placed in the peat pots in the classroom by one person acting as official sower. Each person was told to mark his or her peat pot with the letter "X," "Y," or "Z" for control, blesser, and blighter, respectively, along with his or her initials. The class members were then told to take their seeds home in a brown paper bag and follow these instructions:

Each plant was to be placed in a window with a northern exposure, away from extreme heat or cold. It was to be watered with one tablespoonful of tap water in the morning.

The control plants were to receive no other care. However, the plants in "Y" group were to receive fifteen minutes per day of what we decided to call "blessing." Some had objected to the word prayer, saying that it raised all sorts of presuppositions they didn't necessarily share. But the word blessing seemed to avoid these. At any rate, I pointed out, the thing was to do whatever came naturally.

"Love the plant," I advised. "Get emotionally involved. Praise it, if that seems natural. Encourage it to grow, or, if you prefer, actually pray for it. Project positive thoughts at it."

The plants in the "Z" groups were to receive the reverse —fifteen minutes a day of "blighting." I took pains to reassure some who might have qualms that they need not feel guilty about deliberately trying to inhibit growth.

"There are circumstances in which it is appropriate to try to inhibit or regress growth," I said, "such as in the case of a tumor. If it helps, imagine for the purposes of this experiment that the barley seed is a tumor which you are trying—which you *must*—inhibit. Blast it. Shrivel it with scorn. Picture it being bombarded by a death ray."

If it helped, I said, the blighters shouldn't hesitate to make the seed a symbol of something hated.

"If you can't stand your boss," I suggested, "vent your venom on the seed. You can possibly avoid an ulcer and make a contribution to parapsychology at the same time."

The term of the experiment was fourteen days. At the end of that time the seedlings were brought back to class in brown paper bags. Two procedures followed.

The seedlings were taken immediately to a biologist who, without being told anything about the experiment (the so-called blind method), was asked to measure the plants, root and shoot. (Actually, he did better than that, making no less than five measurements for each seedling: the tip of the shoot to the top of the seed; the tip of the seed to tip of the longest root; the tip of the shoot to top of the root; from the seed to the growing point; and the leaf length above the growing point.)

The measurements were then handed to a statistician, who was asked to go over the figures (without knowing to what they pertained) and note any significant differences among the "X," "Y," and "Z" groups.

There were marked differences among the three groups, the significant one being between the control and blessing groups, on one side, and the blighting group on the other. Taking the measurement from the tip of the shoot to the top of the seed as the normative one, the control seedlings averaged 12.5 centimeters, the blessed ones 12.7 centimeters, and the blighted ones 6.0 centimeters.

These measurements tended to support our hypothesis. The blessed plants grew slightly taller than the control group, but the blighted ones grew less than half as tall as the others. In fact—and this caused the biologist who did the measurements some amazement—62 percent of the blighted seeds did not even germinate. These seeds put out not even the minutest shoots, the biologist remarked, and yet upon examination they appeared to be healthy, showing no fungus or other visible disease. (For purposes of comparison, 16 percent of the control seeds didn't germinate, but not one of the blessed group failed to do so.)

In his report, the statistician said: "For statistical testing purposes the null hypothesis assumed was that both the 'X' and 'Z' group came from the same population.

"However, this hypothesis was rejected and we can conclude that there was a significant difference in the performance of the 'X' and 'Z' group. In fact, there is a smaller risk than 1 in 1,000 that the observed relationship is a purely accidental result."

He added that there was "too small a 'Y' sample to make a firm calculation but I am quite confident that the 'Y' group is different from the 'Z' group."

In other words, the blighted seedlings were dramatically different from the control seedlings, and there was also a difference, though below the level of statistical significance, between the blessed seedlings and the control ones.

As I have said, no scientific pretensions of any sort are attached to this experiment which, because of the smallness of the sample and the problems in standardizing conditions, can only be considered a provisional exploration of a shadowy area.

To me, the most meaningful aspect of our limited experiment was its clear implication that psi-missing and growth inhibition are essentially the same factor, or at least closely related. Maybe this is the significance of the theological doctrine of "original sin"—that many find it easier to generate negative rather than positive emotions. Doubt, dislike, depression—are these more "natural" to most than faith, friendliness, and fervor?

There seems little doubt that we create, to a large extent, our own emotional atmosphere which can generate either positive or negative force. And this force may make the difference between health and sickness, success and failure —even life and death.

SIX

Memory of the Future

Strange as the X-force that heals may be,
its awesomeness cannot compare with the
inscrutable force that probes the future.
Here is provocative evidence that even
time can be subdued by the power of the
mind. . . .

WHEN QUEBEC terrorists kidnapped two public officials in October, 1970, all Canada, and many people around the world, held their breath.

In Chicago, a professional clairvoyante named Irene Hughes brooded on the kidnappings and came up with several predictions of how the crisis would be resolved. Some of these were accurate—a few, astonishingly so.

It was October 5 when James Cross, British Trade Commissioner in Montreal, was abducted by members of the radical organization which called itself the Quebec Liberation Front, or F.L.Q. On October 10 the terrorists struck again, this time seizing Quebec's Labor Minister, Pierre LaPorte.

The abductors demanded certain conditions for the victims' safe return, notably the release of twenty-three co-conspirators jailed for various crimes.

On October 14, while the fate of the two men remained very much a mystery, my friend, broadcaster Robert Cummings of radio station CJCI in Prince George, British Columbia, phoned Irene Hughes in Chicago about the case.

Mrs. Hughes, whom I know well, is a charming attractive, blond lady, with a family, who has a background in newspaper reporting. Her extrasensory perception has been attested by parapsychologist William G. Roll of Durham, North Carolina, who says that "Mrs. Hughes does seem to have paranormal powers." The Cook County Sheriff's office—Chicago is in Cook County—has acknowledged enlisting her psychic help in some difficult criminal cases.

The clairvoyante's initial impressions about the Quebec kidnappings were made live to Bob Cummings over CJCI at approximately 2:20 P.M., local time, on October 14, 1970. These predictions later were rebroadcast by some thiry Canadian radio stations. Tapes of the programs, with the airing dates, are on file in Toronto with the Canadian Association of Broadcasters, which distributed them through its program exchange department.

Here are some of the high points from the transcript of that initial program:

IRENE HUGHES: "The first gentleman who was kidnapped by that radical group . . . I feel that no harm will come to him. However, I feel that physical harm will come to the second."

ROBERT CUMMINGS: "Do you see his death?"

IRENE HUGHES: "I hesitate very much to make such a prediction as that."

ROBERT CUMMINGS: "But you feel his life is in more serious jeopardy than Cross's is?"

IRENE HUGHES: "Yes I do . . . yes I do."

ROBERT CUMMINGS: "Can you get a psychic impression as to the arrest of the F.L.Q. members responsible for the kidnapping of these two?"

IRENE HUGHES: "Well, it's my impression it may be two to three months, Bob. But I feel that within that time an arrest may come. Actually, I would pinpoint the sixth of November. I said two to three months, but I feel some very striking and unusual news may come on that date, the sixth of November of this year."

ROBERT CUMMINGS: "You mentioned that capture is some weeks away; you don't feel, then, that it may be imminent?"

IRENE HUGHES: "I feel that the news coming out in November may indicate that one of them has been

83

caught, or that they [the police]
have a tremendous lead. . . ."

In another interview with Bob Cummings, on October
18, Irene Hughes said she felt James Cross was being
held in a place "a little northwest of Montreal, I'll say
five miles northwest. . . . It seems to me that the place
in which he is is about three stories high, and maybe
four, but I feel that it is three. . . . Actually, it could
be an apartment building. . . ."

The clairvoyante added: "It's very strange but I see
two women involved in that same group."

On October 19, she described the car used by the
Cross kidnap gang: "I have the feeling there is a dark
car; it looks to me like it's a 1962 model because it has
a heavy square back. I have the feeling that it's black,
and somewhat like a Cadillac. . . ."

On November 9, Mrs. Hughes told Bob Cummings in
another taped interview that James Cross would be released by his abductors.

"I feel that within the next two weeks he will be brought
into public appearance. I say public appearance because
I see him with people on both sides of him, indicating
that some major action concerning him, or some major
news concerning him [is involved]. . . . I feel that his release will come very shortly after this."

In the same interview, the clairvoyante mentioned that
the group which kidnapped James Cross had a baby associated with it—"I'm seeing some situation with a child,
a baby, a newborn baby."

The facts?

James Cross was released unharmed, as predicted, on
December 4, 1970. This was about a week later than the
time suggested by Irene Hughes ("within the next two
weeks," she said on November 9). She also had stated
that just prior to his release she saw Cross making some
sort of "public appearance," in a situation with "people
on both sides of him." In point of fact, the kidnappers
insisted on negotiations before releasing Cross and they
were carried out by a Montreal lawyer, Bernard Mergler,
accompanied by a French-speaking reporter. Shortly after
these negotiations, which included guarantees of safe
conduct to Cuba for the kidnappers, Cross was released.

Irene Hughes had said the abducted diplomat was
being held about five miles northwest of Montreal, in a

place three stories high, which could be an apartment building.

Cross was found in a "triplex"—a three-apartment dwelling—in a working-class residential district of Montreal North. The building had three stories, one apartment to each floor.

The clairvoyante's impressions of the kidnap car tallied well with what reporters described as a "decrepit, dark-colored 1962 Chrysler." Irene Hughes had specifically mentioned the year of the car.

Also, the kidnap group did turn out to include two women, one of whom had an infant son, as the clairvoyante had indicated.

Mrs. Hughes' predictions about the Pierre LaPorte case were also strikingly accurate. On October 17 the Quebec Labor Minister was murdered, fulfilling the prophecy of physical harm in his case.

The first arrest in the LaPorte case came on November 6—the date mentioned by the clairvoyante as one on which "striking and unusual news" would break, probably "that one of them [the kidnappers] has been caught." On that date the police apprehended suspect Bernard Lortie.

The remaining trio wanted in the LaPorte case—brothers Paul and Jacques Rose, and Francis Simard—were arrested on December 28, two weeks before the expiration of the time limit ("within . . . three months") mentioned by Mrs. Hughes in her October 14th interview.

Not all Irene Hughes' impressions were accurate. As she continued to reflect on the kidnappings, no doubt at times consciously striving to come up with impressions instead of letting them come freely, distortions crept in. (One professional psychic confided to me that he was sure, in his own case, that "the censor" of the conscious mind, if it obtruded, immediately muddied his clairvoyance.)

At various times Mrs. Hughes seemed to see James Cross being held captive garbed in a hospital gown, or drugged. Apparently these details were wrong.

It seems to me, after studying the transcripts of the interviews, that the clairvoyante got confused when she was prodded by questions. Conversely, her impressions were clearest and most accurate when they came freely and spontaneously—out of the blue, as it were.

Sometimes she seemed to have the right fact in the

wrong context, if you like. Thus, at one point she said she saw James Cross being driven across Montreal in the dark-colored 1962 model car she was in the process of describing—she felt it was happening even while she spoke. In reality, it did happen, but on the day of Cross's release, when he was driven by the kidnappers in that very car to the agreed-upon release point. At another time Mrs. Hughes seemed to have the feeling that Cross might be flown out of Canada and released in a foreign country. What happened was that the kidnappers, not Cross were flown to asylum in Cuba. However, interestingly enough, Cross was released, technically, on foreign soil, since the location in Montreal where he was handed over to the Cuban consul by his abductors had been declared temporarily Cuban territory.

This is not an exercise in special pleading to excuse or explain away the clairvoyante's less successful statements (if indeed any excuse were needed for such a generally brilliant psychic performance), but an attempt merely to put matters in clearer perspective. The fact is that every parapsychologist knows about a characteristic distortion in ESP called *displacement*. It was noted during the early J. B. Rhine card-guessing tests, at Duke University, that some ESP subjects tended to score not on the current card but on the one ahead. This is "forward displacement." Or some consistently scored on the card behind—"backward displacement." This is the process that may have been operating in some of Irene Hughes' impressions, which seemed to show, as I've pointed out, a curious sort of overlapping.

How did the Chicago psychic come up with the amazing, correct information she did get?

Well, one can say either that she was practicing precognition—literally, "foreknowledge," the mind's apparent ability to project itself forward in time—or that she was just guessing. The trick, of course, is to guess right. If you do it often enough, and with this kind of specificity, you might as well call it precognition.

That Irene Hughes was doing something more than blind guessing is strongly suggested by the fact that she made more than one precise hit. Granted, if she had plastered the wall with a hundred different dates written on scraps of paper, and then thrown darts at them while blindfolded, she might have hit November 6. But what about the other hits? Put together, these indicate a clear tendency on the psychic's part to make correct, detailed guesses about the future. Anybody can make one brilliant guess in a lifetime, but only a psychically gifted person can keep on doing it.

The ability of some people to guess correctly far above chance was put to a careful scientific test by Dr. Helmut Schmidt, formerly a senior research physicist at the Boeing Scientific Research Laboratories in Seattle. His experiments were reported, with favorable editorial comment, in the October 16, 1969, issue of *New Scientist*, a respected British journal.

What Dr. Schmidt did, in effect, was to devise a sophisticated guessing game based on the behavior of electrons.

Why electrons? Well, the answer to that involves what is called quantum theory. There is an accepted scientific doctrine (so my physicist friends tell me, my own state of knowledge on the subject approaching what theologians used to call "invincible ignorance") that the behavior of electrons in relatively small numbers is random and therefore unpredictable. If, for example, a chunk of radioactive substance were placed near a radiation detection device, it would be impossible to guess with more than chance accuracy the moment when an electron would be registered. The electrons are hurled out of the radioactive substance purely at random.

It seemed to Schmidt that a definitive test, then, for precognition would be to ask people to try to guess the moment when the next electron would register its arrival on the radiation detection instrument. He devised the following experimental setup. A small piece of strontium-90, a radioactive element, was placed near a Geiger–Mueller tube, an electron-detecting instrument. This was connected to an electronic four-position switch rotating at the rate of a million steps per second. This in turn was hooked up to four different colored lights which corresponded to the four positions of the switch. There were four colored pushbuttons corresponding to the lights.

If a button was pressed, nothing happened immediately. But when the next electron struck the Geiger–Mueller tube (the rate of emission was about ten electrons per second) the rotating switch stopped in whichever of the four possible positions it happened to be at that moment, and the corresponding colored light came on.

The challenge for the subject in the experiment was to guess which colored light would come on next. If he guessed the red one, say, he pressed the red button. If the red light came on next, he had scored a hit; and other colored light would indicate a miss.

Since the arrival of each electron was automatically registered on a tape, as were the subject's guesses, the possibility of human error in recording the test results (a frequent object of criticism in ESP experiments) was eliminated. The score was computed by comparing the two taped records.

Helmut Schmidt did a series of preliminary experiments, using approximately a hundred subjects. Most of them obtained chance scores, but there were some notable exceptions. One consistently high scorer was a physicist, identified only as Dr. D. W., who told Schmidt that his dreams often came true.

For the main experiment, Schmidt turned to a group of professional psychics in Seattle, including a well-known spirit medium, Keith Rhinehart. In 63,000 individuals trials, Rhinehart and two other self-styled psychics got significant scores. In fact, the probability of obtaining such high scores by chance was less than one in 500 million.

These were striking results. But they got even better when Schmidt conducted a second series of experiments, this time replacing the now unavailable Rhinehart with a sixteen year-old girl who said she was developing ESP. In this series, Schmidt asked the subjects to vary their performances, aiming at an above-average score on one run, and a below-average score on another. In the first instance, the subject was told to press the button corresponding to the colored light that would come on next; and in the latter instance, to press the button corresponding to any light that would *not* come on next.

Out of approximately 20,000 trials the subjects got very significant scores, the odds against chance being 10 billion to one.

With odds such as these it is unthinkable, according to the mathematicians, that chance alone was responsible. What was the crucial factor?

Was there possibly some mechanical bias in the instruments? Did the rotating switch, for instance, have a queer propensity to stop more often at one position than another, thereby establishing a pattern which an astute subject might have detected?

Schmidt ran through no less than 5 million trials with

Micronite filter.
Mild, smooth taste.
For all the right reasons.
Kent.

© Lorillard 1973

America's quality cigarette.
King Size or Deluxe 100's.

Collect the Kent "Collectables."

Take advantage of this special Kent offer. Order these attractive items for your family and friends.

the same button activated over long periods of time to find out if this yielded extra-chance scores. Result: "A computer evaluation of these numbers did not suggest any, even temporary, deviation from the theoretically expected randomness," he said.

What about cheating?

I mention this last refuge of the incurably skeptical mind simply because allegations of fraud have, in fact, been made against ESP researchers from time to time. Cheating, conscious or unconscious, on the part of subjects and experimenters, was suggested as an explanation of significant ESP scores by American physicist George Price in a 1955 article in *Science*, the issue recently has been resurrected by a British critic, psychologist E. G. Hansel.

However, in an automated experiment such as this one, the possibility of trickery by the subjects seems rather convincingly ruled out. As to the question of cheating by the experimenter—well, such a suggestion is wholly gratuitous in the case of a respectable scientist and wouldn't even be mentioned in any field less controversial than parapsychology.

To me, the conclusion is unavoidable: The subjects in this experiment did indeed guess the behavior of electrons with phenomenal accuracy. To do this, they must have read the future.

Since, according to all the evidence, ESP emerges from the deep layers of the mind, in most people only sporadically surfacing into conscious awareness, it isn't surprising that one form in which precognition often comes is dreams. These, after all, are what Freud called "the royal road to the unconscious."

Many people have, at least infrequently, dreams which appear to be prophetic; some people have them more or less regularly. (Probably more of us have them than realize it, since, as dreamologists tell us, the average person remembers only one dream out of a hundred. Significantly, several people I know who started keeping dream diaries—records of their dreams which they make a habit of jotting down immediately upon awakening—report having striking precognitive experiences, whereas formerly they rarely recalled dreaming at all.)

An unusual precognitive dreamer is Mrs. Gwen Bridgland, a clergyman's daughter and English housewife who lives near London. She has been studied over a period of time by parapsychologist John Beloff, head of the psychology department at the University of Edinburgh, who vouches for the fact that some of her dreams have contained definite futuristic material. One of the most striking concerned a bizarre suicide.

In a letter which Mrs. Bridgland sent to Professor Beloff, postmarked September 5, 1969, she described a dream which at the time she felt certain was precognitive. In this dream, as Beloff reported, she "saw a man throwing himself under a train and somehow knew that he was wanted for a sex murder."

On September 19, a man hurled himself in front of a train from a railway platform in the British county of Hertfordshire. On December 31, the *London Times* reported that the police were convinced that the suicide victim was the man wanted for a sex murder committed in Hertfordshire on September 16, some two weeks after Mrs. Bridgland's dream.

Professor Beloff commented: "The whole incident is not merely coincidence. It is not every day—or even every year—that a man wanted for a sex murder dies under a train in a dream, and a man fitting the same description dies under a train in real life."

London Times reporter Brian Cashinella said that he interviewed the precognitive housewife in January, 1970, and asked her to describe the man in her dream.

"She described exactly the man who was killed under the train," he allowed. "This description had never been published but after I talked with her I checked the description with the coroner's court. Everything tallied. She had described the man's hair style, the brown jacket, the flannels—even the green turtleneck sweater he wore. I was very impressed and amazed at her story."

The spontaneous evidence for precognition, provided by cases such as Mrs. Bridgland's, converges with laboratory evidence. Together, they establish the credibility of the phenomenon. However, even the most cogent evidence fails to break down the resistance of some skeptics. The reason is that precognition seems impossible to fit into any sort of conceptual framework which makes sense to modern science. Even some parapsychologists have confessed that they can't swallow precognition without acute intellectual dyspepsia. One such parapsychologist, William Roll, suggested replacing the idea of precognition with that of a kind of anticipatory psychokinesis (or PK—the mind's apparent ability to influence matter at a distance). In this view, the successful prophet shapes circumstances, by unconscious PK, to make them conform to his prediction.

According to this concept, the subjects in the electron-guessing experiment did not really foretell the behavior of the electrons, but *created* that behavior. . . . The prophecy was father to the fulfillment; when the subject predicted that the red light would come on next, his own PK caused it to happen.

Obviously it would be very difficult to show that Schmidt's work does indeed indicate precognition rather than PK. What it comes down to is a balancing of the two hypotheses against each other and a choosing of the one which appears to be more plausible in the light of all the known data.

In spontaneous cases it seems easier to show that precognition is more plausible, in some instances, than PK. In Mrs. Bridgland's case, for example, the PK interpretation says that her unconscious mind forced the man she dreamed about to commit that sex murder and then throw himself in front of a train. (Actually, such mind-to-mind contact or influence would be telepathy, not psychokinesis.) Strange as precognition may be, the PK view here sounds even stranger to me.

Can we really believe that when Irene Hughes predicted physical harm would come to Pierre LaPorte, she caused that harm to come about? Or that her unconscious PK was powerful enough to have arranged for the first arrest in the case to occur on November 6? Anybody who can believe this, it seems to me, can believe anything. Why not precognition?

To be sure, there no doubt are such things as self-fulfilling prophecies. (I mean besides the obvious examples in which a person, say, told by a fortune-teller that he will become a great success, is thereby motivated to go out and make the prediction come true). It is conceivable that a prophet, predicting that a certain person is going to commit suicide, could dominate the person into the deed by telepathic suggestion. PK, rather than telepathy, would come into play if the prediction involved a physical object, as in the mechanical failure of an automobile.

However, it should be kept in mind that the pygmy PK thus far demonstrated in the laboratory—most such effects show up only as deviations from a statistical norm, as in dice-throwing experiments—is a long way indeed from the giant PK needed to invoke railway accidents, shipwrecks, volcanic eruptions, earthquakes, and similar events, which have been accurately predicted.

Admittedly, the logical and philosophic objections to precognition are formidable, but some at least provisional answers are possible.

For example, it is argued that if a future event causes a precognitive experience (which presumably is so), we have the anomaly of an effect happening before its cause. This runs counter to all commonsense notions of causality.

Well, it is a safe rule that in matters of ultimate importance common sense is often wrong. The familiar cause-and-effect relationships appear to break down not only on the level of precognitive experience but on the microphysical level of quantum physics. Psychoanalyst Joost de Merloo (in the *International Journal of Parapsychology*, Autumn, 1968) quotes the distinguished nuclear physicist Werner Heisenberg as describing "the reversal of time relationships when under the circumstances of meson physics the explosion of an atom nucleus occurs before the causative disturbing particle is there. According to Heisenberg, the usual unidirectional order of time sequences between cause and effect is reversed."

Another common objection of precognition maintains that since the experience is, by definition, a knowing process, it must have an object (the thing which is known). But in precognition the object of the knowing process is a future event which does not yet exist. Therefore, we have the anomaly of a knowing process with a nonexistent object.

One reply to this objection is that the past, in a certain sense, doesn't exist either, yet memory is a fact. Surely the blow that was struck last week, the precise emotional reaction that was experienced, the words that were spoken —these are no longer in existence in the way that they were during the moment they happened. But who, on that account, would deny that memory of these events is a genuinely knowing process?

Some theories of precognition imply a future that already exists, which undercuts these objections. However, this view raises problems of its own. One is free will.

If the future already exists, says the argument, then it must be as immutable as the past. And this makes free will an illusion. The clothes you will wear tomorrow, the break-fast you will eat, the words you will utter—these must be predetermined if the future has already happened. This makes the future, for all of us, not a play whose lines are scripted in advance, which would be bad enough, but some-thing worse: a play already filmed, in the can, waiting to be screened.

Well, *is* the future already in existence, as a sort of not-yet-experienced present?

The empirical evidence on this point, it seems to me, is ambiguous. Certain evidence suggests that the future is plastic and can be manipulated by an act of will in the present. There are documented accounts concerning people who experienced premonitions of some disaster which, by heeding the premonition, they were able to avert. This certainly seems to show that one can change the future.

Typical was the vivid dream of an immense ship sinking which induced an English businessman, J. Connon Middle-ton, to cancel his reservation on the ill-fated *Titanic.* (The case is described in Martin Ebon's book, *Prophecy in Our Time,* New York, New American Library, 1968.) Of course, one could argue that Mr. Middleton's apparent premonition was part of his predetermined future and that therefore everything happened exactly as it was planned.

The idea of a pliable future which can be reshaped to some extent, before it hardens irrevocably into the present moment implies that precognition is a form of exalted or glorified inference. The deep mind, computerlike, can amass, sort, and assess the total of present possibilities and from these extrapolate what is going to happen. On the basis of this forecast, the provisional future can be changed so that, for example, if you are heading for a watery grave next Tuesday because you're booked to sail on a doomed ship (doomed by a structural flaw, let us say), you can avoid that fate by switching to another ship.

Attractive as this view of inferential foreknowledge may be, however, there are cases which it doesn't seem to fit. In the experiment with the electrons, the results do not appear to be attributable to any sort of inference because, as far as science knows, the electrons exhibited no pattern, however subtle or hidden, from which their future be-havior could have been inferred. Schmidt's work illustrates what I have come to think of as true, or classic, pre-cognition, in contrast to quasi-precognition.

Quasi-precognition would cover all those cases—some types of which we've already taken a look at—which appear to be genuine foreknowledge but, on closer examination, can be more plausibly interpreted as other forms of extrasensory activity. This includes instances in which PK influence, or telepathic suggestion, may have caused a predicted event to happen. Or cases in which plain telepathy or clairvoyance are mistaken for precognition. An example of this would be an instance in which a psychic predicted somebody's death based on the extrasensory awareness that the person had a mortal disease. If you know that somebody is terminally ill, it doesn't take precognition to foretell his demise.

True precognition seems to me to be very much like memory. As a matter of fact, F. W. H. Myers, the great classical scholar who was one of the founders of the Society for Psychical Research in London, called it "promnesia"—memory of the future. The word is richly suggestive. Consider some of the features which memory and precognition appear to share.

Memory is not infallible (though, of course, it's infinitely more efficient than precognition, just as ordinary perception in general is infinitely more efficient than ESP). Even the memory of a single, well-defined event is rarely, if ever, perfect. There are characteristically gaps, distortions, and sometimes even bizarre aberrations in the remembering process. Generally speaking, the further away in time the recollected event is, the less precise the recollection.

Similarly, in precognitive experiences, events far in the future seem to be perceived more dimly, as a rule, than those which are nearer. There are exceptions. Both in memory and in precognition, an event which holds special importance for a person may be perceived with greater clarity than an unimportant event much closer in time.

Memory can be altered by our wishes, hopes, and fears, and so, presumably, can precognition. Just as our hopes may throw a glamour over the past, they may do the same to the future. And if our fears can blot out painful memories, perhaps they can obliterate (at the conscious level, anyway) painful precognitions. This may account for cases of apparent precognition in which certain features are brilliantly clear and accurate while others are curiously hazy or distorted. (Numerous psychics have told me, for instance, that they cannot foresee their own destiny—a censoring mechanism seems to come into operation if they try.)

The idea of precognition as a form of memory offers a possible way of resolving the conundrum of free will versus determinism.

The usual argument, as we've noted, is that if our future is mapped out in advance it must be predetermined. And this demolishes free will, making us mere automata going through the motions of being free while in reality our every choice already has been made, our every deed already done.

But is this argument valid? Does the idea of a mapped-out future necessarily imply such absolute determinism?

For example, if a prophet yesterday foresaw my wearing today the red tie I am in fact wearing today, does this prove that I *had* to wear the tie in question, that I had no choice in the matter? Many people, it seems, would say yes. But let's look at it a little differently. Keeping in mind the analogy of precognition as memory, consider the concept of the past. The past represents something which is mapped out, which cannot be changed, yet this doesn't imply determinism. Who would care to argue that the fact that I wore a red tie yesterday proves that I *had* to wear it? This doesn't follow in logic at all.

If, then, we think of the future as a pattern of events which is already, in some sense, past, why should this mean that that pattern of events was predetermined?

Some thinkers about time have suggested the concept of a "specious" or "prolonged" present, meaning that what is past and future to us may, from another vantage point, be the present. Some subatomic particles have a life of a fraction of a second; their whole past, present, and future is crammed into one moment of our time-scale. If we had the means of perceiving events happening to that subatomic particle, they would all seem to be taking place in the present.

Similarly, is it not conceivable that at some "higher" level of reality our future is as much past—right now—as our past is to us in our normal experience? Could precognition represent a breaking through to that other level of reality to glimpse the future as something which, from that vantage point, has already happened?

The fact that a prophet can foretell what kind of lunch I will eat tomorrow does not necessarily mean that my choice of lunch will not be free, any more than the fact

95

that I can tell you what kind of lunch I ate yesterday means that that choice was not free.

To end this excursion into frank speculation, let me cite what may be a familiar, but nonetheless singularly useful, illustration of what we've been considering.

April 14, 1912, was indeed a night to remember. At 11:40 P.M. on that date, the *Titanic*, the biggest luxury liner afloat, on her maiden voyage from Southampton to New York struck an iceberg and sank.

With her, and the proud myth of her unsinkability, went down as estimated 1,517 persons.

In his definitive account of the first and final voyage of the *Titanic* (*A Night to Remember*, New York, Holt, Rinehart and Winston, 1962), Walter Lord mentions that a writer named Morgan Robertson created a novel about a huge, opulent Atlantic liner, loaded with rich and complacent people, which, during an April voyage, hit an iceberg and sank with virtually everybody on board. The name of Robertson's fictional ship was the Titan, and it had been proclaimed unsinkable.

Besides the name, and the circumstances under which the ship sank, there were obvious parallels between the fictional vessel and the *Titanic*. Both ships were equipped with too few lifeboats; the *Titan* had 3,000 persons aboard and 24 lifeboats, the *Titanic* 2,207 persons and 20 lifeboats. Both ships had a top speed of 25 knots. In the novel, the vessel's displacement was 70,000 tons, while the *Titanic*'s was 66,000 tons. The fictional liner's length was 800 feet, that of the *Titanic* 882 feet. Both ships had three propellors.

Obviously, Morgan Robertson's novel was a rewrite of the story of the *Titanic*, and not too imaginative at that. The only trouble with this theory is that the novel was published in 1898—fourteen years before the wreck of the *Titanic* and several years before that glittering ship was built. Instead of the familiar fiction based on fact, we seem to have here fact based on fiction.

Coincidence?

Or, with so many specific analogies, memory of the future?

PART III

The Outermost Limits:
Life After Death

SEVEN

"Ghosts" Who Write
Letters & Pose
for Portraits

*If the mind conquers time, can it also
defeat death? And if so, and the dead
survive, can they communicate with us,
the so-called living?*

AS I watched, the elegantly dressed, white-haired
English lady propped the large black fountain pen between
her thumb and forefinger—not gripping it but cradling it
there—and, in a moment, the pen moved.

Slowly, shakily, it wrote: "I'm here . . . Gordon Burdick."

This was May, 1967, and Mr. Burdick had been dead
for ten years.

I was paying a return visit to Grace Rosher, the London
artist—her miniature portraits have been hung at the
Royal Academy—who receives automatic writing purportedly inspired by her fiancé, the deceased Gordon Burdick.
(He died in 1957, on the eve of his departure for England
to marry Miss Rosher.)

Before proceeding with this narrative, let me make it
plain that one of the occupational hazards of the psychical researcher is being inundated with communications
from people, often enough little old ladies with blue hair,
who claim to be in touch with the seventh astral plane.
Most of this material which I've had the dubious pleasure
of examining has been tendentious drivel; rarely has it
exhibited the intellectual level of even a fairly bright
twelve-year-old. Certainly, none of it struck me as evidence
for communication from the dead.

As a rule, 99 percent of the stuff received via the Ouija
board or automatic writing is an obvious extrusion from
the unconscious—or conscious—minds of the people involved. Rarely, the material shows evidence of genuine

ESP at work, but even more infrequently is there any substantial indication of a source outside the focal person.

Actually, as many as four out of five people can develop automatic writing, according to psychiatrist Anita Mühl, an authority on the subject, quoted by Leslie M. LeCron (in his book, *Self-Hypnotism*, Englewood Cliffs, N. J., Prentice-Hall, Inc., 1964). In many cases all that's needed is that the person sit quietly, hold a pen or pencil loosely in his hand, and try to make his mind a blank; sooner or later, with a little patience, the pen begins to make wiggly lines, then it may write words, shakily but legibly. Throughout the procedure the person is often certain that he is not moving the pen.

There is nothing in the least supernormal or even abnormal about this. It is simply an example of what psychology calls automation—behavior, sometimes quite complicated (as in sleepwalking, where the somnambulist may get out of bed, go downstairs, and bake a cake without awakening), accomplished without the awareness of the conscious mind. Automatic writing (or automatic drawing, even typewriting) is a way of tapping the unconscious levels of the personality. The surrealist prose spewed forth by the seemingly autonomous pen comes from the writer's own inner self and can provide significant clues to his mental and emotional state. Sometimes the automatic script is exotic, even bizarre; it may take the form of mirror writing, or the words may be written backwards, or a new language may be invented for the occasion. All this can be interesting to a psychoanalyst.

If you have gathered that I'm not impressed by the psychic possibilities of most automatic writing, you are not mistaken. However, Grace Rosher's case, which I first personally investigated in London in 1965, seemed to me to merit a second look for several reasons.

First, a professional graphologist (a handwriting analyst, such as the courts use in forgery cases), F. T. Hilliger of Surrey, after studying samples of the deceased Gordon Burdick's calligraphy and the automatic script declared that the latter "was, if it were humanly possible, genuinely inspired by the personality of Mr. Burdick." And second, Miss Rosher had a wrinkle which set her apart from most automatists in the matter of technique: the pen wrote for her while merely cradled between her thumb and forefinger, as I've described, and on occasion even while simply propped against the outside of her clenched fist.

Moreover, a number of thoughtful and perceptive students of psychic phenomena, such as Britain's Sir Victor Goddard, had gone on record as considering Grace Rosher's automatic writing to be strong evidence for communication from the dead. (See Goddard's foreword to Grace Rosher's book, *Beyond the Horizon*, London, James Clarke & Co., Ltd., 1961.)

On my first visit to Miss Rosher at her home in the London borough of Kensington, I had found her to be a charming, alert woman, obviously in possession of all her faculties and not, it seemed, given to florid fantasies. As a matter of fact, she expressed in no uncertain terms the aversion to "dabbling in the occult" which she had felt all her life until, unbidden, the Burdick scripts started.

"I was never given to peering into crystal balls or anything like that," she sniffed, and I believed her.

But, as she told it to me, her own occult visitation started on a day in September, 1957, soon after the sudden death of her fiancé, Gordon Burdick, in Vancouver; apparently he had suffered a heart attack in his sleep. It was in the midst of writing a letter to some friends to tell them of Gordon's death that Grace Rosher suddenly heard, as she put it, an inward voice which said, "Leave your hand there and see what happens."

Her instant mental reaction was, Why nothing is likely to happen. But to her astonishment an electric pulse seemed to pass through her hand, which was resting idly on the page, loosely holding the pen; then the pen began to move without her conscious control.

As Grace Rosher watched, feeling like a bystander, the pen slowly and shakily scrawled: "With love from Gordon. . . ."

That was the beginning of a phenomenon which has produced hundreds of pages of automatic script purporting to emanate from the spirit world. The ghostly Mr. Burdick seemed very quickly to get the hang of writing with somebody else's hand ("I place my etheric hand over yours and guide it," the scripts assured Grace Rosher), because soon the pen was moving fluidly across the page, tracing his characteristic handwriting.

Though by far most of the material was said to originate with Gordon Burdick, a few other people communicated directly, too. More often, Gordon passed on messages from others in his world (members of Grace Rosher's family, for example) and, on occasion, conveyed messages the other way—from his medium to somebody no longer on the earth plane, as Spiritualists put it.

It was a few months after the phenomenon started that Grace Rosher one morning took a hard look in the mirror and asked herself if she was going out of her mind or, indeed, already had gone. How could she, a proper High-Church Anglican who had always thought Spiritualism slightly lower class, really believe that she was getting letters from a dead man—and in his own hand?

She even expressed her doubts to her spectral correspondent, saying: "This seems too good to be true." The pen replied: "Nothing is too good to be true. . . ."

But the uncertainty remained, so Grace Rosher, in her crisp way, decided to find out if she was nursing a fantasy. Bundling her automatic scripts together, she hied herself to the Reverend Maurice Elliott, an Anglican clergyman who was then secretary of the Churches' Fellowship for Psychical Study (now slightly amended to the Churches' Fellowship for Psychical and Spiritual Studies). This is a sort of cerebral ghost-hunting club for the likes of Church of England bishops, eighteen of whom, at last count, were members.

The Reverend Mr. Elliott responded with distinctly modified rapture when Miss Rosher dumped her missives from the other side on his desk.

"He told me that they got an awful lot of automatic writing and most of it was rubbish," Grace Rosher recalled with a twinkle in her eye.

The next morning, however, she received a phone call from Mr. Elliott; he sounded like a man who had stumbled across buried treasure.

"Well, it certainly isn't your writing," he allowed, "and it definitely *is* his."

With Grace Rosher's permission the automatic scripts were submitted to Mr. Hilliger, the graphologist previously mentioned, along with specimens of her normal handwriting and Gordon Burdick's from life. The graphologist peered at the specimens through a microscope and concluded, for a starter, that the automatic script *hadn't* been written by Gordon Burdick. At any rate, not while he was alive. The "stroke"—the actual trail of ink left by the pen—was different from that in letters he had written before his death, said the graphologist. But he had some further, more interesting, observations.

Though the stroke was Grace Rosher's, he declared,

the automatic script was in all other respects virtually identical to Gordon Burdick's handwriting. In fact, he identified sixteen out of twenty characteristic features of Burdick's calligraphy which were reproduced in the scripts —a phenomenon without precedent, he said, in his experience.

Could it be a clever forgery?

No, said Hilliger, adding: "It is well-nigh impossible for a human being in the conscious state of existence to imitate or 'draw,' without actually tracing another person's handwriting, for any length of time, a series of forgeries as consistent in so many respects. . . ."

(Note, however, the phrase "in the conscious state of existence," which may provide a clue to an interpretation of the writing I'll consider later in this chapter.)

Reassured that she wasn't mad, and that other intelligent, disinterested people were inclined to accept the automatic writing as being what it purported to be, Grace Rosher settled down to enjoy her almost daily interworld correspondence.

The scripts said that Gordon Burdick had fallen asleep in his bed in Vancouver and awakened in a beautiful garden with flowers that were like enormous shimmering jewels. He had no idea where he was until he saw his mother and several of his brothers and sisters, arms outstretched, coming toward him. Then he knew that he was dead.

At first, Gordon admitted, he felt regret at having left the earth plane, mainly because it meant separation from his fiancée. It was his mother, apparently, who reassured him by pointing out that communication with the before-death state, though difficult, wasn't impossible. Gordon said that he decided then to manage it, if it was at all possible. The automatic writing was the result of this decision.

The world described in the scripts is very much like this one (too much so, for some people's tastes). In general terms it accords with what many other respected mediums have described. It is a type of existence, apparently, in which people's mental states are translated into objective reality; they create their own environment. Gordon Burdick said that he was on the first plane of spirit existence, just slightly beyond the earth plane, really. Beyond him were at least six other higher spheres, he reported, but there were also several sublevels—depressed areas, as it were. After death, he pointed out, people gravitate to the plane which corresponds to their level of spiritual development.

The souls on the lower levels, explained Burdick, were not consigned there by divine decree but simply because it was the place where they would feel most at home. The higher spheres, one gathers, might be as hellish for these people as a concert of Wagner probably would be for the average devotee of hillbilly music. (Emanuel Swedenborg, the great Swedish mystic and seer, observed that God lets people go to hell because He loves them and knows they would be miserable anywhere else.)

The discarnate Mr. Burdick confided that he spent a great deal of his time doing "rescue work"—assisting newcomers to the spirit world to adjust to their unfamiliar circumstances, especially those disoriented by a sudden or violent death. Many of these refused to believe they were dead, and some needed treatment in "rest homes" where, after alternating periods of therapeutic slumber and wakeful growing awareness, they came to accept their new state.

Gordon Burdick, according to the scripts, also practiced a sort of social work among the astral down-and-outers on the lower planes. It was only through self-effort that these underprivileged souls could better themselves, he explained.

"The place itself is unspeakably dreary and gloomy and there seems no beauty or peace there," say the scripts about one of these basement areas on the other side. "The trees are stunted and the country devastated-looking—no birds or flowers. . . .

"The people there must come to realize that they are solely responsible for their present state, that it is not God who is inflicting it on them but that they have punished themselves; that it is the law of cause and effect operating in its inexorable way and that it is up to them to find a way out of this condition by changing their attitude to life and other people."

Such sermons as these punctuate the Grace Rosher scripts; they may reflect her religious background as well as the fact that Gordon Burdick had been raised a Christian Scientist.

At one point, the spectral Mr. Burdick was so busy helping newcomers from a rash of plane crashes that he left Grace Rosher in the middle of a sentence and the pen didn't move again until the next day. On his return, he snapped: "So many crashes! What is the matter with these aircraft?"

Life after death, as the purported Mr. Burdick describes it, does appear to be very much like life after birth. "We eat for sociability or pleasure," one communication said, "not for sustenance."

Love continues, according to the scripts, but "as a mental affinity which attracts like minds. There is a mating of minds here. . . ."

This may not appeal to everybody, but the scripts give the assurance that "the spiritual fusion is satisfying on a higher level."

Religious services continue over there, apparently, for those who want to participate. The religion espoused in the scripts is a kind of liberal Christianity. Christ is described as "divine" but not as identical with "the Divine Mind." However, "he is honored above all others."

Touching on cosmology, the scripts opt for the theory of continuous creation: "Creation is a perpetual unfolding of what already exists in the Divine Mind."

What about ethical concepts among the spirits?

Questions on these subjects elicited answers not unlike those one might reasonably expect from a person of Gordon Burdick's background. Certainly, the comments evinced no overwhelming moral grandeur (although one wonders what evidence of that would be).

Asked if capital punishment was right or wrong, the pen, apparently manipulated by the unseen communicator, replied: "I think it depends on the circumstances in connection with the crime. Some forms of crime are such that the danger to other people, especially children, is greater and more serious than the removal of the criminal by death."

In reply to a question about whether humane execution was better for the criminal than a life term in prison, the scripts proposed an idea which some people will find alarming: a therapeutic death penalty—therapeutic, that is, for the criminal, not for society.

"Some of those who commit dreadful acts, especially against children, are themselves being used by evil minds on this side who seek to gratify their own horrible desires by projecting them into the minds of certain persons who are open to these influences," the scripts claimed. "If this kind of criminal or maniac is freed from the physical body he ceases to come under the influence of the evil ones on this side and has a chance to become a normal being. . . ."

In one communication, Gordon Burdick summed up: "The whole spectrum of human life continues here, from the sublime to the ridiculous."

Some may find the world he depicts too banal, too middle-class for their liking (it was George Bernard Shaw who remarked that he wanted to go to hell since all the interesting people seemed likely to be there). Certainly the scripts do not betray any hint of remarkable intellectual stature, or of the saving grace of humor. But then, they themselves stress that the purported Mr. Burdick is describing only what he has experienced, and this has been molded by his personality, hopes, expectations, and, yes, limitations. The communicator expressly disclaims any quasi-omniscience, insisting, rather, that he is only one step ahead of the rest of us on the so-called earth plane.

By Burdick's own statements that thought creates environment in the after-death state, it is maintainable that there are as many next worlds as there are inhabitants of them. Some parapsychologists, such as H. H. Price of Cambridge University, have suggested that post-mortem existence could take the form of a sort of dream state in which we experience a procession of images and sensations as we do in dreams. Interaction with the dream worlds of others might come about by telepathic interplay among like-minded spirits.

One reason for my return visit to Grace Rosher was to see what I hadn't had an opportunity to witness the first time—the actual phenomenon of the pen writing without apparent control by the automatist. This time I observed the phenomenon and photographed it.

I sat next to Grace Rosher on an overstuffed sofa in the dark-paneled parlor of the apartment she shares with her sister. She had a clipboard such as college students use to take notes during lectures propped on her knee and several sheets of blank note paper. She cradled the man's style fountain pen between her thumb and forefinger and the nib rested on the paper. The pen lay there, inert; we waited. . . .

After a few minutes of intense concentration on Miss Rosher's part, the pen stirred and then scrawled, as I've said, in an uneven hand: "I'm here. . . ." A moment later, it added: "Gordon Burdick."

There was a pause of possibly a minute before the pen wrote again, still shakily: "Will someone ask a question?"

Dutifully, I inquired as to whether there were any other unseen presences in the room besides the presumptive Mr. Burdick—hopefully, someone I knew.

"I am not aware of anyone else present," the pen replied, still shaky.

It felt a little odd talking to a pen (for that's what it seemed like), but the feeling quickly passed. One can get used to the strangest things.

There were obvious problems. The pen wasn't performing well enough to suit Miss Rosher. She was very apologetic about its snail-like pace and the spidery writing which suggested somebody afflicted with palsy.

"I don't understand the mechanics of this business at all," she said, a tone of exasperation creeping into her voice. "I don't know why it works. I don't know why sometimes they'll do very well and at other times very badly. But that's always been the case. This is a disgraceful performance, let me tell you."

The pen seemed to shrink under her scolding. I reassured her that it was doing just fine, and the unusual ritual proceeded.

"Is this difficult for you?" I asked, addressing the pen. "Yes," was the reply, scrawled slowly. "It needs very great concentration. I am not in very good form tonight."

Really, I thought it was performing very nicely indeed for a pen writing without any obvious assistance from the woman against whose finger it was balanced. But to liven things up a bit I wondered aloud whether it might not be better for the automatist to try holding the pen normally and see what happened. First, however, could we get another specimen of the communicator's signature without the pen being gripped?

"Signature, please," snapped Grace Rosher.

The pen quite rapidly traced, in firm, clear handwriting: "Gordon Burdick."

When the automatist held the pen normally, as she did for the rest of the session, it wrote briskly.

I asked just what the mechanics were in automatic writing.

"Well, it is like this," the script replied, "I take the pen and try to guide it by the psychic power I have acquired. But at present I must be in contact with the physical vibration of my assistant. . . ."

106

At this last word, Grace Rosher, who was watching the pen apparently with as much interest as my own, laughed: "Assistant? Well, he's never called me that before."

A sly dig, I wondered, for the scolding a little while ago?

"You see," the script continued, flowing smoothly now, "we are obliged to lower our own vibration to the physical level, which is not at all an easy thing to do. It requires a great deal of concentration."

Had he, the communicator, ever written through any other medium?

"Only once," was the reply. "That was several years ago when a foursome was requested by the graphologist."

"Yes," interjected Grace Rosher, "that was very interesting indeed."

At my request she told me about it.

"It was an experiment in what's called cross-correspondences," the automatist said.

In the summer of 1959, at the request of Mr. Hilliger, the graphologist, a certain lady from the U.S.A. —her name was Mrs. Florence Pell—tried an experiment with me in exchanging our spirit controls.

Her husband, a clergyman, had passed on fourteen years before and she had been receiving communications in automatic writing which was remarkably like his handwriting. It was arranged that one afternoon I should ask my communicator to find Mr. Pell on the other side and bring him to write through me, while Gordon Burdick was to write through Mrs. Pell.

The session began and I noticed that while Mrs. Pell appeared to be getting writing that looked like Gordon's I was getting only row after row of very tiny squiggles. At last I said, "Whatever's the matter with Mr. Pell? He can only produce squiggles!"

Then we found that Mrs. Pell always held the pen firmly, whereas I was just resting my fingers lightly on it as I did when my own communicator was writing. As a result poor Mr. Pell couldn't control it. As soon as I gripped it tighter, extremely small writing like the squiggles appeared, and it was writing with which I wasn't in the least familiar.

In regard to this cross-correspondences experiment, the Reverend John Pearce-Higgins, vice-provost of London's

Southwark Cathedral and vice-chairman of the Churches' Fellowship for Psychical and Spiritual Studies, received a letter from graphologist F. T. Hilliger on September 28, 1961, stating: "I confirm that prior to this experiment, so far as I am aware, it was beyond the bounds of possibility for Miss Rosher to have had sight of the handwriting of the late Mr. X on the one hand, and for Mrs. X to have had sight of the original script of Gordon Burdick on the other." Yet the graphologist, apparently, was satisfied that the automatic scripts, through these different mediums, resembled their respective originals.

I asked the pen if there would be a third World War.

"I am afraid there may be," it wrote. "But whatever happens, this country of England will not come under fire as in the last war."

Can dwellers in the other world routinely see into the future?

"We can see further than you," was the reply, " but only for a few months ahead. Those who have progressed to higher spheres can see further still, but I am only on the first plane of experience over here. Even so, we can see further ahead than you can and also further into the past."

This answer reminded me of a comment on the nature of prophecy by the trance-personality of James Wilkie, a mediumistic friend of mine. He likened the after-death state and the heightened vision it gives to standing on a mountaintop overlooking a wide valley, which is this world of time and space. Events, both past and future, stretch out below the mountain like a vast panorama and those which are furthest in the future appear dimly, as distant objects would. The closer to the present the future events are, the more clearly they can be discerned.

This analogy is reminiscent of what I called the "prolonged present" in Chapter 6, Memory of the Future. From a high enough vantage point, beyond the ordinary time-space continuum, the past, present, and future may be seen as equally present, one vast now.

I suggested bringing the automatic writing session to a close with a simple psychological game-test—a word association experiment in which the pen would write whatever come to mind (Gordon Burdick's or Grace Rosher's mind, of course, not the pen's) when I mentioned certain key words.

The theory was that if the surviving consciousness of

Mr. Burdick was guiding the pen, it ought to respond in ways quite different from Grace Rosher's.

At first, Miss Rosher seemed not to get the point of what I was suggesting; then she caught on and agreed, with a little diffidence, to try it. She felt, I suspect, that my idea was a little silly, but she was being a good sport about it.

I said: "Georgia."

The pen immediately wrote: "British Columbia."

This seemed an anomalous response, until I asked Grace Rosher if by any chance Gordon Burdick had lived in the Georgia Hotel in Vancouver.

"Why yes," she replied, "I believe he did."

I said: "Ships."

The pen wrote: "A lot in the war."

Burdick's family, it appears, was in shipbuilding and had big navy contracts during the Second World War.

I said, "Eddy."

The pen wrote: "Mary Baker."

Gordon Burdick was raised as a follower of Christian Science, of which Mary Baker Eddy was the founder.

I said: "Bennett."

The pen wrote: "Never met him."

I had in mind W. A. C. Bennett, the prime minister of British Columbia; Gordon Burdick died before the gentleman took office.

The responses were interesting but too fragmentary to be much more. Whether they even suggested the influence of a mind other than Grace Rosher's was moot, since she knew Gordon Burdick so well. Properly used, however, the word association technique might have real value in trying to distinguish between the medium's personality and that of a purported communicator.

How good is Grace Rosher's automatic writing as evidence of human survival after death?

Well, as far as the actual technique of the writing is concerned—the pen leaning against her fist—this, though dramatic, is not in itself supernormal. After my visit with Grace Rosher I tried it myself. Using a clipboard tilted toward me on my lap, as she had done, I was able to write with the pen balanced between my thumb and forefinger. The handwriting was spidery but legible. A friend of mine tried the same experiment and found that he too could do it. Though it looks hard, it is apparently a skill most people can pick up with relative ease.

I'm speaking here of the pen propped between the thumb and first finger. On numerous occasions, apparently, Grace Rosher practiced her automatic writing with the pen simply balanced against her loosely clenched fist. In several photographs, the pen is writing in this fashion while the automatist sits at a flat-topped desk, not with a clipboard on her knee tilted toward her (which seems to make the performance easier). The Churches' Fellowship for Psychical and Spiritual Studies made a motion picture of the pen writing rapidly propped against Grace Rosher's fist. This is more impressive, in terms of the actual modus operandi, than what I witnessed.

Even this style of automatic writing may not be really unusual, however. Simeon Edmunds, a British psychical researcher, in his book, *Spiritualism: A Critical Survey* (London, Aquarian Press, 1966), denies that a pen writing while balanced on one finger is at all special. He reproduces a photograph of a young man apparently performing the feat. However, we are not told what sort of script the man was able to produce in this manner, or how long he was able to keep it up.

Grace Rosher told me that originally Gordon Burdick said that he was working toward total control of the pen on his part, without any physical contact. In other words, the pen would hold itself perpendicularly and write merrily away while, say, Grace Rosher sat by doing her knitting. The closest she got to this state of affairs, she maintained, was when once she held the pen suspended by a piece of string and it wrote, shakily: "Gordon Burdick." I got the impression that Grace Rosher does not now expect the phenomenon of the fully autonomous pen to come about.

As a matter of fact, I suspect that the phenomenon is waning somewhat. This would not be unexpected. The automatism started some fourteen years ago and the medium is getting on in years; typically, mediumistic abilities fade with age.

How significant is the reproduction of Gordon Burdick's idiosyncratic handwriting?

This, no doubt, is a genuinely curious manifestation. Handwriting is among the most individual of human activities; it's almost a fingerprint of the personality. The question is whether the duplication of a person's calligraphy in this way argues necessarily for spirit agency.

The graphologist Mr. Hilliger, you remember, stated his opinion that no one "in the conscious state" could so closely mimic another's handwriting. But what about someone in an unconscious state? To put it another way, somebody whose unconscious mind was in control?

Very few people, if any, could consciously reproduce their own handwriting as it was when they were six years old. Yet psychologist Leslie M. LeCron says that a hypnotically regressed adult can produce writing which is "almost identical when compared with actual specimens of the subject's childhood writing." (See *Experimental Hypnosis,* edited by Leslie M. LeCron, New York, Citadel Press, 1965.)

Grace Rosher was intimately familiar with the handwriting of Gordon Burdick for many years and the mimicking of it which she does, though presumably beyond her conscious skill, may not be beyond the resources of her unconscious.

But what about instances when the automatist reproduced handwriting she had never seen?

In the cross-correspondences experiment, when Grace Rosher and Mrs. Pell switched communicators, both ladies, it appears, were able to reproduce the other's automatic script with a high degree of accuracy. Mr. Hilliger, the graphologist, vouched for the fact that Miss Rosher hadn't seen the "squiggly" handwriting of the late Mr. Pell.

On another occasion, she received communications purporting to come from Sir William Crookes, the great nineteenth century physicist and psychical researcher. Maurice Barbanell, editor of London's *Psychic News,* ferreted out a rare specimen of Crookes' signature from life and it proved to match closely the signature appended to the automatic script (a fact I was able to confirm for myself by examining and comparing the two).

Could these phenomena be explained in terms of the unconscious mind's masquerading powers, creating a facsimile of the personality of Gordon Burdick, plus ESP in the medium? Her knowledge of the handwritings of the late Mr. Pell and Sir William Crookes may have come through clairvoyance (Crookes' signature was in existence and therefore accessible to supernormal perception) or telepathy (Mr. Pell's calligraphy could have been picked up from his wife's mind).

Granted, such as ESP faculty—that is, one capable of reproducing idiosyncratic handwriting—would be startling, but we do not know the limits of extrasensory awareness and theoretically it is possible.

On the other hand, unless one rules out a priori the possibility of life after death, there is the alternative explanation: that Gordon Burdick, Mr. Pell, and Sir William Crookes, among others, are still alive in another dimension and have communicated through Grace Rosher's automatic writing.

The phenomenon of "ghosts" writing, if the Grace Rosher case was really an example of that, was not so curious as my next mediumistic experience: "ghosts" who sit for their portraits.

Mrs. Coral Polge (this is her professional name; she is married now to Tom Johanson, a well-known British Spiritualist leader) specializes in sketches of the departed who, she says, obligingly model for her. In May, 1967, I visited the "psychic artist" in her home in the London suburb of Twickenham. Tall, dark-haired, and attractive, Mrs. Polge knew nothing about me; the sitting had been booked in the name of Mr. Allen.

We had barely shaken hands when the medium said she strongly felt the presence of "some relatives of yours, your maternal grandparents, I think," and fairly rushed me to a chair. Seizing a pencil and a sketch pad, she started drawing at a furious rate. As the pencil flew over the page, Mrs. Polge gave me a running commentary on my grandparents whose spirit forms, she said, were visible to her standing behind my chair.

"This is your grandfather," she murmured, glancing up only occasionally from her sketching. "He seems to have had sore feet. Must have walked a lot."

I smiled—he was a postman.

"He was a little downtrodden by his wife, you could say. . . . He couldn't manage money, but he was very kind-hearted. . . . Liked his wee nip now and then. More than a wee one, sometimes. . . ."

None of this was startling but it was, as far as I was concerned, accurate. Though I had never seen my grandparents, my mother and father had told me a lot about them.

The sketch, which was finished in less than five minutes, seemed to me to bear so remarkable a likeness to a photograph of my grandfather that I gasped (although the photo I had in mind was taken twenty years or so before my grandfather's death and therefore looked much younger than the medium's sketch). There was the drooping mustache, the finely shaped nose, the high but not receded hairline. As far as I could see, the man in the sketch was definitely an older version of the man in the photograph.

Coral Polge ripped off the top page of her sketch pad and started another drawing. This, she said, was my maternal grandmother. Again, she gave a verbal description while she sketched.

"She was a strong-willed person," the medium muttered, absorbed in the sketch. "Very strong-willed."

This certainly accorded with what I had heard about my grandmother.

"She had a shrewd business sense and really did remarably well in a financial way, though she had little enough to start with."

This, too, fit.

Then, as the medium completed the drawing, she held it up with a flourish for me to see. It was a striking likeness of my grandmother. Most striking were the firm, almost tyrannical set of the jaw and the tight, no-nonsense mouth. That was grandmother all right, as I had come to think of her.

Then the medium said: "Just a moment. She asks for one little change."

Erasing the mouth, the medium redrew it—softer, this time, with a hint of a smile. The transformation was dramatic; the face now was still formidable but at the same time almost cherubic.

"She says she wants you to know she wasn't as bad as she sometimes may have seemed," the medium said.

I confess I chuckled, although I'd been trying to keep a straight face to avoid providing the medium with any sensory clues that might have helped her with the drawings.

Mrs. Polge then went on to do seven more sketches, none of which meant anything to me, with one exception. There was a North American Indian (inevitable, it seems, in every séance), an elderly Chinese gentleman (said by the medium to be one of my spirit guides), a very old lady wearing an old-fashioned sleeping cap, a mustachioed middle-aged man, a young girl, an older man with a rather nondescript face—and my mother.

The last sketch was a near success but didn't quite make it. As the medium sketched, I watched her accuracy with increasing appreciation—it did look like my mother's face emerging. Then, subtly, the sketch diverged into something which was more a likeness of me than my mother. Was the medium, wittingly or unwittingly, basing it on my appearance, assuming that there was a mother-son resemblance?

And if so, could this sort of family resemblance theory explain the likenesses of my grandparents? I didn't think so.

However, knowing the human tendency to project into things what we are looking for (this is the key to the ink blot test), I wondered if the likeness to my grandparents was only in my mind. Would others also see it?

As soon as I arrived home, I got a partial answer, at least. Without giving my wife, Marion, any inkling of what I was up to, I took the two sketches out of my suitcase and held them up.

"Your grandparents," my wife said immediately. "Where on earth did you get these?"

After a determined search we dug up the old photograph of my grandmother and grandfather which I remembered had hung in my late parents' home. Placing the photo and the sketches side by side, Marion and I agreed that there was a distinct—we felt astonishing—resemblance.

Could it be coincidence?

To test this, I took all nine sketches the medium had done and lined them up on a table next to my grandparents' photo. Ten people were asked to pick the two sketches from the nine that matched the photograph. All ten picked the sketches of my grandparents. The resemblances my wife and I saw, then, were not merely in our minds.

Many people have agreed that there is a marked resemblance between the sketches and the photograph. Some have argued that such a likeness couldn't possibly be accidental. But not all have had this reaction.

Eugen Fandrich, an instructor in social sciences at Ryerson Polytechnical Institute, Toronto, professed to see no "striking resemblance" between the medium's drawings and the photo.

"Is the medium merely skilled at drawing the faces of older people," he suggested, "and, after seeing you, simply sketched what she thought your grandparents probably looked like?

"Or am I biased against seeing any resemblance as you may be biased in favor of seeing one?"

He proposed a brief experiment in which I agreed to cooperate.

"Without telling my students what I planned to do," Mr. Fandrich said afterward, "I asked them to bring to class the following day any photographs of their grand-

114

parents they had available. I received four photographs of men and five of women. Three days later I conducted the following experiment.

"These were my instructions to the students: 'Last week I collected a number of photographs of grandparents—including some from this class. An artist has made a sketch of one of the men and one of the women in these photographs. I would like you to match the artist's sketch with the photograph of the person and list the reasons for your choice.'

"The photographs, including that of Mr. Spraggett's grandparents, were arranged on the desk in sequence from the smallest to the largest. With Mr. Spraggett's photo included, there were five of men and six of women.

"The sketches were placed below the photographs."

The results of the experiment?

Thirty-six students took part. Eight of them chose the photo of my grandfather as the one which best matched the sketch of the man. Statistically, the probability that a student would select my grandfather's photo by chance was 20 percent; in actuality, 22 percent of the students made that choice. This was hardly above chance. At the same time, sixteen of the students chose another photo; and nine, still another. The indication, then, was that any resemblance between the photo of my grandfather and the sketch was more imagined than real.

In matching the sketch of the woman, twelve out of thirty-six students chose my grandmother's photo. Twenty-four students split their votes unevenly between two other photographs.

The probability that the students would choose my grandmother's photo by chance was one out of six, of 17 percent. The actual response was twice that—twelve out of thirty-six, or 33 percent.

In his conclusions, Eugen Fandrich stated: "By far the majority of students chose another photograph rather than that of Mr. Spraggett's grandparents as the one that most closely resembled the sketch.

"This experiment did not prove that the sketch had no likeness to the photograph of Mr. Spraggett's grandparents, but only that, in the opinion of the majority of students, there were other persons who more closely resembled the sketch."

However, a statistician who went over the data noted that they indicated a pronounced above-chance resemblance between my grandmother's photograph and the medium's sketch. This resemblance was expressed by the fact that twice the number of students expected by chance alone picked my grandmother's photo—two out of six instead of one out of six.

The statistician computed the odds against this response being due to chance as a hundred to one. These odds, he pointed out, are considered sufficient to establish statistical significance in medical research. In other words, statistically, the likeness between the medium's sketch and my grandmother's photograph was not accidental.

For my part, given the accurate verbal descriptions of my grandparents with which Mrs. Polge accompanied her sketching, I believe her art probably does have an extrasensory element. Like most mediums—or, for that matter, anybody else—her performance no doubt is uneven. I've seen sketches of hers which seemed to me to be less than successful matched against the corresponding photograph. Of course, one of the problems is that a great many people have a great many points of resemblance to a great many other people. The most striking likenesses are bound to be those in which the subject happens to have an idiosyncratic feature—a peculiar scar, say, or an eye patch, or eyebrows in the shape of inverted "v"s.

One of the most successful of Coral Polge's psychic drawings is reproduced in Maurice Barbanell's book, *This Is Spiritualism* (London, Herbert Jenkins, 1959). It is a truly striking likeness of the deceased J. P. Hutchinson of South Harrow, Middlesex, judging by an accompanying photograph of the dead man. In fact, the drawing appears to have been sketched from the photo. However, the subject's widow swore a declaration before a commissioner of oaths that the medium, Coral Polge, never saw any photographs of her husband until after the sketch was completed.

In this case, the family resemblance theory—that the medium simply draws what she thinks the subject looked like based on the appearance of the relative who's present —breaks down, since it doesn't apply between husbands and wives.

Another suggestion is that the psychic artist has an uncanny knack of reading unconscious clues provided by the sitter's reactions to the sketch. A raised eyebrow

116

might mean, to the medium, that the jaw in the drawing isn't quite right; a frown, that the nose is a trifle too large, and so one.

This theory wouldn't apply in cases where there is no physical contact between the medium and somebody who knew the subject of the sketch. Some psychic artists, such as Frank Leah of London, are said to have made sketches successfully from contacts over the telephone.

Coral Polge apparently has been successful at this psychic drawing over the telephone. She said she once received a request through the mail from a dead boy's mother. The woman returned the first sketch, saying simply it was "Not quite right," and asked the medium to try again. The same thing happened the second time. At the third attempt, the drawing matched the boy's photograph—which the medium hadn't seen—perfectly. (Here, of course, one would like to know exactly what was said over the phone to determine if any clues were given the psychic artist.)

Coral Polge says that in point of fact she doesn't usually "see" her ghostly subjects (although sometimes she does) but "senses" them in a way that is hard to describe. "I sense only the personality linking with me," she has said. "For a few moments I become totally different, taking on the patina of the tired old lady or the frightened child communicating, and knowing how they tick."

(There is no doubt that one of the problems in this field is human gullibility—the almost universal tendency for people to see what they want to see—or, conversely, not to see what they don't want to see. A case very much in point was reported in the June 6, 1970, *Psychic News*. John Cochrane, of Hertsfordshire, England, was reported to have sent duplicate drawings to people as "psychic" sketches. Three people gave *Psychic News* drawings they had received from the artist and the three "duplicate" each other, the Spiritualist newspaper said.

A significant fact is that, until this situation came to light, some people were satisfied that the artist had provided evidential sketches for them. Tommy Heyburn of Bangor, Northern Ireland, for example, said that Cochrane did a sketch for him which he recognized as his spirit guide, Dr. Angus. It was this picture which two other people also received.)

If Coral Polge can, on occasion, produce noncoinci-

117

dental likenesses of deceased persons, does this indicate human survival after death? Do the spirits of the departed model for their drawings, as the medium claims, or does she read her sitters' minds?

In my case, I had in mind the old photograph of my grandparents. The medium could have been picking up these images in mind. To be sure, this would be pretty sensational ESP, but it wouldn't necessarily point to human sirvival after death.

On the other hand, if Mrs. Polge, as I've already suggested, were able to produce accurate likenesses of people unknown to anybody in her presence, routine telepathy certainly would be ruled out. The explanation might be clairvoyance, by which the medium tapped the minds of people not present, or even mentally scanned photographs buried in an attic somewhere. But this, if it happened, would hardly be less amazing than survival.

My feeling is that people like Coral Polge possess an unusual and picturesque kind of psychic ability—one which, properly tested, might indeed yield vital evidence bearing on the issue of life after death.

Anyway, I hope my grandmother liked her picture....

EIGHT

The Amazing Music
of Rosemary Brown

*From past-mortem literary endeavors to
spirit composing is not a surprising transition. But the otherworldly music said to
emanate from a band of celebrated composers certainly has surprised the skeptics. . . .*

IN OCTOBER, 1970, I had tea and muffins and a
wonderful chat with a lady who is one of the strangest
musical mysteries of our time.

Her name is Rosemary Brown.

She is a London widow in her late forties with two
children, so poor that she didn't have a radio until 1965,
and her roof still leaks. She has amazed British musical
circles by creating some five hundred compositions in
the exact styles of such masters as Liszt, Chopin, Schubert, Beethoven, Debussy, and Rachmaninoff.

The really crazy thing is that though Mrs. Brown's
music is good enough to have made her at least a mini-
celebrity, she is a musical novice with extremely limited
formal training. Her piano technique is improving, she
says, since Rachmaninoff started giving her lessons (he's
been dead for thirty years, of course), but she still can't
play many of the pieces she writes.

Actually, she insists that she doesn't write the pieces
but merely takes them down, note by note, like a stenog-
rapher. And those who have watched her at her composing, such as British musicologist Dr. George Firth, say
that taking dictation from some unseen person is exactly
what she appears to be doing.

A claim of receiving musical dictation from deceased
composers takes some believing, of course. But the reaction of many of Britain's musical elite to Mrs. Brown
has been—well, respectful.

Richard Rodney Bennett, an eminent young composer,

admitted: "I am absolutely fascinated by this music. You couldn't fake it without years of training. I couldn't have faked some of the Beethoven myself."

Hepzibah Menuhin, sister of violinist Yehudi and a concert pianist in her own right, confessed: "I regard these pieces with immense respect; each one is distinctly in the particular composer's style."

And pianist Louis Kentner, a well-known Beethoven authority, playing one of Mrs. Brown's ghostly sonatas on British television was so unnerved by its "incredible" likeness to the master's work that he exclaimed: "I hope there's some rational explanation."

For the past two years Mrs. Brown has received from the Scott Fund—a trust set up by admirers of her music —a weekly stipend of four pounds, sixteen shillings (about $12.00). This allowed her to give up her job in a school kitchen and devote all her time to composing.

Rosemary Brown, I discovered when we met, is a disarmingly simple woman with a silvery laugh. She is totally charming. Most people who have met her, even hard-core skeptics, have found it impossible not to believe in her utter sincerity. She tells her extraordinary story as though it were the most ordinary experience.

We chatted about her improbable career in the parlor of her distinctly unpretentious Victorian terrace house, in the London working-class district of Balham, where she was born and still lives.

"Where does your music come from?" I asked her directly.

She laughed and brushed a stray wisp of reddish-brown hair out of her eyes.

"Well," she said thoughtfully, "I have no doubt it is coming from a source outside myself.

"I can't myself compose. I've tried to, without any assistance from the spirit composers, but I can't get even a tune, and I certainly wouldn't know how to harmonize it.

"I think agreement is fairly unanimous among the experts who've studied the music that I couldn't be creating it."

Rosemary gave a self-deprecating shrug.

"There are so many composers communicating—more than a dozen—that it does seem impossible for any person to write hundreds of pieces of music in their styles.

"I have had it said to me that even a fully trained musician wouldn't be capable of going on like this, turning

120

out one piece after another. Most are piano pieces but I've also gotten violin sonatas and string quartets, about a dozen Schubert songs, and two unfinished symphonies by Beethoven."

I asked the world's most unusual composer exactly what the extent of her musical training was.

Well, I had a few piano lessons as a child. Then there was a break and I had another two terms in my teens that I paid for myself. There was a long break and then I had just over a year of lessons before I got married.

There was no general musical background because we were a very poor family, which meant that we couldn't go to concerts or recitals, and there weren't classical records in the house for me to listen to. So I didn't have listening experience.

There was a period of about twelve years, after I got married, when I dropped music entirely. The composing didn't get started until after my husband passed over into the spirit world in 1961. And even then nothing happened for some years because I had to go out to work. I had two very small children to care for and I had no time or energy to do anything else.

But in 1964 I had an accident and injured some ribs, which meant that I was laid up at home for some weeks. And I think Liszt found that this was the opportunity to begin his work. He straightway began to give me music.

It wasn't quite as sudden as this account might suggest. Mrs. Brown explained that she was psychic from childhood and often saw and heard things others couldn't. When she was seven, a spirit with long white hair and a flowing black cassock told her that he was a composer and that one day he would make her a famous musician. Rosemary said she didn't know who he was until, in her teens, she saw a picture of Liszt.

Liszt's return visit started a procession of spirit composers.

"Not very long after Liszt came, he began to bring Chopin," Rosemary Brown said, as matter-of-factly as if she were discussing the neighbors dropping in.

Liszt introduced Chopin as he might have if they

121

were coming for tea, rather like that. It was quite a formal business, really.

For a long time I used to call him M'sieur Chopin because I thought perhaps that was the appropriate title. And then one day he said to me, "What is all this M'sieur Chopin, why do you not call me Frederic?" And so then I tried to call him Frederic. But still sometimes I think it's a bit familiar.

Next were Schubert and Beethoven. They came more or less together. Schubert still seems to have very great admiration for Beethoven and I think rather tends to follow him about.

The next, I think, was Bach, and I believe Brahms was next. Then I think it was Schumann. I'm not quite sure of the order. But we progressed on to Debussy and up to Rachmaninoff. He's the most recent who has given me any quantity of music, although I've had limited contact with a few more modern composers.

How do the composers convey the music?

"Liszt began simply by guiding my hands at the piano," Rosemary said. "This is rather like the technique of automatic writing. I almost felt as if somebody was putting my hands on like gloves and then playing through them.

"I didn't understand what the music was, I wouldn't even know what key it was in. I used to learn through the pattern of the notes on the keyboard. I simply knew whereabouts I'd got to put my hands next."

Sometimes Schubert would sing one of his songs, Rosemary mentioned, "but he hasn't got a very good voice.

"Then I began to realize that I wouldn't be able to remember the music, as from just a dozen pieces it grew to a hundred, then two hundred."

Gradually, the composers switched to dictating the music, giving their earthly collaborator the key, the timing, the left hand, the right hand.

"It took quite a time for the dictation stage to happen," she admitted. "I had to get used to working with the composers and perhaps they had to get used to working with me. When Rachmaninoff first came there was almost hostility between us. I don't know why. But that's gone now and I am grateful for the help he's given me with my piano technique.

"I graduated from where my hands were guided at the

122

piano to the system of oral dictation we use now most of the time.

"When I get to the final score, Beethoven, who's very fussy, will go through it in detail. Liszt doesn't seem to worry as long as I have got it down. Bach is usually so clear and sure that I get it right the first time; it's a mathematical process, almost, with him."

What about personality differences among the composers?

"Oh, they're very different," Rosemary replied with a quick laugh,

extraordinarily different. Bach, I should think, is at one end of the scale, to use a musical term. He seems a very subdued person in his outward speech and behavior and dresses in quiet colors. He's a very strong personality but almost dour.

At the other extreme is Debussy who's a very colorful person, almost a hippie. He comes wearing bizarre clothes—sometimes a straw hat or a huge cravat hanging down almost to his knees.

Chopin is very sympathetic, a very kindly sort of person, and with quite a lot of gaiety. Liszt is a very devout person, really.

Haydn is very kindly, almost a father figure. I haven't any music from him but he did try to help me with my playing.

Beethoven terrified me at first because he looked very fierce and sullen. And of course it's natural to be over-awed in the presence of such great souls. But gradually I've become more at ease with him so that I will now sometimes venture to ask one or two questions, although it's usually only about music. I couldn't talk to him freely as I do Liszt or Chopin.

They often joke with me. If they think I'm downcast they try to cheer me up.

How do her spectral collaborators look to Rosemary Brown?

"They all appeared older the first time they came but now they look to be about thirty-five. Liszt is dressed in the style of the late nineteenth century, sometimes with a very colorful cravat, sometimes with more somber clothes.

"At times I can see him as clearly as I can someone who's here in this dimension. Sometimes the vision is blurred, or fades out altogether. The same with their voices—sometimes as clear as a bell, at other times they fade like a foreign station on the radio, or when there is a bad connection on the telephone."

The composers speak mainly in English, which Rosemary doesn't find odd ("Why shouldn't they have gone on learning on the other side?"), but lapse into German or French when excited. *"Mein Gott!"* Beethoven exploded when they were in the midst of a composing session and the doorbell rang.

Once, during a similar session with Chopin, the composer burst out in excited French: *"Le bain va être englouti!"* He kept shouting this until Rosemary realized he meant the bath (which her daughter had left running) was about to overflow; she rushed upstairs to turn it off.

"We've been very good friends since that incident," she confessed with a shy smile.

Liszt speaks very good English, "although in a stilted manner. Occasionally he doesn't know the English equivalent of something and then he'll use a German word, or perhaps French, instead."

I asked Rosemary Brown which composer was her favorite as a person.

"It's very difficult to say," she replied earnestly. "But I do think perhaps Liszt is nearest to my heart because he's worked so patiently with me and he's tried to help me, not only to improve my playing but to understand some of the fundamental things of life, the great questions of religion. And these are things I'm very deeply interested in.

"The reason for this mediumship, you see, is to show people evidence for life after death. It's not a question of communicating more music as much as trying to establish communication with the spirit world, and to establish without any doubt that it is these composers communicating."

At this point an interesting interlude occurred. Rosemary Brown suddenly said that Debussy was in the room, "he's standing right behind you."

I asked how he looked.

"He's wearing a sort of tam-o'-shanter," the medium informed me, obviously amused. "And he's also got a very long cravat which is of the same material, sort of multicolored. He's wearing the tam in sort of an artist's style, a little bit rakish."

"I'm interested in Debussy," I allowed. "I know very little technically about music, but I've been enormously moved by his music and there's one piece I'm particularly interested in, one of his nocturnes called *Festivals*. There's a sequence in that, which I call the caravan sequence, which is exciting but seems unlike Debussy's other music. It builds up to a thrilling crescendo, where his other music tends to be more delicate and impressionistic. Does Debussy think this is his best piece, I wonder?"

"I'll see if I can get him to comment on this," Rosemary replied. She starred intently over my left shoulder for a moment. Then she spoke, deliberately, rather haltingly, as one who was interpreting a foreign language might speak.

"This piece of music you mention I don't know at all myself. Debussy is saying that one of his—he's saying it in French and I'll have to try to get it translated—his favorite piece personally is something called *Nuages*.

"But, to try to explain the other piece, he says he was feeling in a very fatalistic mood, as if everything was horribly predestined and there was this relentless march of time which was carrying everything forward whether it wanted to be carried forward or not. So it was very much a piece of music of his mood at that time."

Why was *Nuages*—in English, *Clouds*—Debussy's own favorite?

"He says he feels this is a happier piece of music and also more of the universe. It expresses more of life itself, ebbing and flowing. The other piece, he feels, was a more artificial type, perhaps more of the intellect than of the heart."

I mentioned that I'd often felt that the word which expressed best the quality of Debussy's music was "shimmering." Was he happy with that word? How would he describe his music?

The reply was somehow very much what I felt Debussy might have said: I could imagine him bowing slightly as he spoke.

"Yes, he says this is a beautiful word but, alas, he doesn't feel he always shimmered very well.

"He says he sometimes felt very weighed down and now, looking back on his music, he feels it sometimes becomes heavy because of his own depression of spirit. But really, within himself, he is more of a lighthearted nature. These were only passing moods."

Did Debussy have any criticism of the way his music generally is performed?

"He has said to me often that his music is played rather

poorly from the point of view of interpretation," Rosemary informed me.

"The technique may be correct but the interpreter doesn't enter into the spirit of the music. Debussy thinks people must let themselves go far more when they play his music. There should be much more color and movement in his music. Because all the time he felt that life was surging movement, and it was color and change in colors, and this should come out in his music, this feeling of something living and moving."

Since the composers have stated that the purpose of their interworld collaboration with Rosemary Brown was not to add to the body of their music but to convince people of survival after death—of the composers' personal survival—I asked if they were satisfied with the results.

"Well, they feel that on the whole they're having a much greater degree of success than they originally hoped for," the medium said.

"They find that human consciousness is opening up; young people nowadays are beginning to inquire into these questions, and very often in a sensible way. People are not satisfied with just a material life, they're beginning to want something more. And so they are responding very well to this attempt to break through to them from the other side."

If composers continue composing after death, does this mean plumbers keep plumbing and architects go on designing buildings? What about undertakers—are they out of a job?

Rosemary Brown laughed and her eyes twinkled.

"Well, perhaps the undertakers could help in conducting people from our world into the next," she suggested. "Instead of burying people, resurrect them, as it were.

"Actually, there's always great scope over there for people to take up something that interests them, which is also giving service. If you have any talents which you haven't been able to develop in this life, well of course you have the opportunity there to do so. This is a wonderful thing for people who were denied the opportunity here."

"Are you sure that you personally are going to live after death?" I inquired.

"Oh, quite sure," she said, in the tone, I thought, of a patient mother explaining something to a rather slow child. "I was certain of this long before the music started.

"This is something I can't prove to anyone but I can remember distinctly being alive before coming into my present body. Memories of waiting to be born.

"I'm sure everyone survives death, whether they want to or not. It's an automatic process. Some people, perhaps, go with more difficulty into the other life, but they go."

To conclude our conversation, Rosemary said that she wanted to play for me two pieces from the other side— a prelude by Chopin which came in July, 1970, and a scherzo Beethoven gave her in August of that year.

As a musical innocent I can't comment on the pieces' technical quality, but I thought the Chopin brilliant and vivacious, and the Beethoven passionate and complex. The music moved me.

Did these compositions actually emanate from two composers who shuffled off this mortal coil a very long time ago? Are they still creating melodies and harmonies in some rococo music room in the sky, or the astral equivalent thereof?

Some critics have doubted this because of what they contend is the generally substandard quality of the music.

Alan Rich, the music critic of *New York* magazine, after hearing some of Rosemary's recorded music, professed to be unimpressed. He commented:

If this record is on the level, we can forget once and for all that old legend about composers dying before their best works were written. If this stuff is all Bach, Chopin, Schubert and the others can dredge up to send down to earth, it looks very much as if they've spent their time up in Heaven doing a lot of second-rate rewrite jobs on some of their better-known compositions. Maybe the Life Up There is too easy; artists must suffer, you know.

Take the two pieces by Bach. The first is just a haircut (and not too much off the top) of the Prelude in C Minor from *The Well-Tempered Clavier* (Book 1), almost measure for measure. . . .

The other pieces are similar reworkings, although the two by Beethoven and Schubert are a little more imaginative in that they combine a lot of pieces in one hodgepodge, instead of sticking to just one. Thus, the Schubert starts off with one of his German dances, sticks in a bar or two from Who Is Sylvia and then goes tromping around through other Great Hits before coming to an awful bump for an ending.

That's very untypical; Schubert himself may have come to an early end but none of his pieces do. The Beethoven mostly uses one of his early "easy" sonatas (Opus 49, No. 1) with a wad out of the finale of the *Appassionata* sonata somewhere in the middle, like a lump in the mush.

What interests me is that almost all the composers have sent down works that were characteristic of their early-period styles. I know we're supposed to be reborn when we get to heaven, but don't we ever get to grow up again?

In contrast to Mr. Rich, who used to be music director for a radio station, Richard Rodney Bennett, regarded as one of Britian's leading young composers, said of Rosemary's work: "Even if some of the pieces are bad, that doesn't mean anything. I produce lots of lousy pieces.

"We can all imitate Debussy at the piano if we want to, but to create a piece of music—which is coherent as a piece of music—which seems to go very much to the roots of the composer's style by re-creating it instantly, is much more complicated. People tend to minimize the importance of notation and the difficulty of notating what one actually wants to hear, but in general [Rosemary's] notation is extraordinarily assured and competent. She does get down on paper exactly what she wants to hear and from working with my own students I know how difficult this is. . . ."

Pianist Louis Kentner, who allows that there is a remarkable similarity between Mrs. Brown's style and Beethoven's, suggests, as do some psychiatrists, that the medium may have a phenomenally retentive unconscious mind and that the music "derives from her memories of the various composers' works."

But Rosemary claims to have had virtually no memory of the composers' works on which to draw.

"I didn't know Liszt at all," she said, "except for the *Liebstraume* and one of the Hungarian rhapsodies. I had never played Brahms or Rachmaninoff; I knew only one piece by Schubert and no Debussy except for *The Little Shepherd*. One of my teachers tried to get me to play Bach but I didn't like him; I was surprised when he came because I thought surely he knows I am not a Bach fan. But that didn't bother him; apparently he simply put it down to my lack of musical eduation."

The medium insists that when Chopin first came she didn't even know he was Polish and took down his words phonetically. Later somebody identified them as Polish.

Is it possible that Mrs. Brown is really a musical genius who, for some inscrutable reason, is hiding it?

Mary Firth doesn't think so. Mrs. Firth, wife of Dr. George Firth, a musicologist and former director of the Scotland Arts Council, and herself a noted musician and lecturer, studied Rosemary Brown closely in the early days of her composing.

"I gave her ear tests and sightreading," Mrs. Firth reported, "and all the miserable things that teachers give to students. I discovered, largely to my surprise, that she didn't seem to have a basic music ability such as I would have expected in any student, and certainly in a student doing compositions. In other words, I could play a simple melody which she simply couldn't take down. When I played two simple parts these were utterly beyond her."

Mrs. Firth also examined a scale which Rosemary said Liszt had given her for practice, and some piano exercises from Brahms.

"It is one thing to write down pieces in the style of well-known composers," she commented, "but quite another to produce a new scale with pieces to match and some fingering exercises. In the latter case, Brahms, as every pianist knows, is one of the most awkward composers to finger properly."

On Mrs. Brown's grasp of Liszt's style, the comments of Humphrey Searle are significant. Searle, considered one of Britain's leading Liszt authorities, examined the Rosemary Brown–Liszt composition *Grubelei*. In a letter dated London, September 2, 1969, he said:

> This is a very interesting piece, though it doesn't exactly resemble any piece of Liszt's that I know— apart from one bar which I will come back to later on.
>
> It is the sort of piece which Liszt could well have written, particularly during the last fifteen years of his life when he was experimenting in new directions.
>
> One very remarkable point is that most of it is written in ⁵⁄₄ time against ³⁄₂ . . . this sort of thing was not common in the 19th century. . . .

"Grubelei" is defined in the dictionary as "meditation" or "musing" and the piece certainly had this character. The markings in the score are mainly in Italian, according to Liszt's usual practice, though there is one in French, *"avec tendresse,"* which is also in character. . . .

This is an extremely interesting piece, whoever it is by, and we must be grateful to Mrs. Brown for making it available to us.

Searle's remarks about the piece reflecting Liszt's late period contradict Alan Rich's criticism that the music was typical of the composer's early work.

I asked Rosemary herself about the criticisms that the music was uneven in quality. Did this sort of stricture bother her or her ghostly mentors?

"I think the quality of the music varies according to the quality of the communicating," she said thoughtfully. "I think, as I've mentioned, that the composers are interested primarily in communicating the fact of survival rather than in getting some great piece of music across. I don't think they worry about criticism."

Actually, some musically sophisticated people have received what they consider remarkably useful tips from Rosemary—hints which seemed to reflect accurately the style and knowledge of the particular composer purportedly communicating.

Richard Rodney Bennett said he visited the medium and told her he was having trouble with one of Debussy's preludes, but did not mention which one. Rosemary promptly passed on some advice from Debussy which apparently proved very apt: ". . . vary the tempo, use more pedal."

Professor Ian Parrot, who teaches music at University College, Aberystwyth, Wales, is inclined to agree that "any flaws [in Rosemary's music] are due to her problems in communicating. Writing down a symphony is almost a superhuman task. Poor Beethoven would probably find it virtually impossible to give it to her."

Mrs. Brown told me that the composers are always patient with her, even the gruff Beethoven, but that sometimes, when trying to dictate a symphony, he simply "gives up and quietly goes away for a while."

My friend Stewart Robb has made a careful personal study of Rosemary Brown's mediumship and is planning a book about it. Robb is an expert—a musicologist, concert harpsichordist, opera librettist (he's the authorized translator of Wagnerian operas for the Metropolitan in New York)—and he took a degree in concert piano from London's Royal Academy of Music.

For those who are inclined to dismiss what Rosemary Brown does as merely an interesting curiosity, Robb stresses that a composer's style is almost as idiosyncratic as his fingerprints and to imitate it exactly is an "incredible" thing.

"There have been attempts by even brilliant musicians to imitate the style of another but they never fully succeed," Robb told me.

"Schumann wrote a little collection of gems called *Carnaval,* in one of which he tried to simulate the style of Chopin, but you can hear Schumann unmistakably gleaming through.

"Back in the 1930s I myself heard some pieces allegedly discovered by Fritz Kreisler which were supposed to be forgotten works by the eighteenth century composer Pugnani. When I heard them I was sure they weren't Pugnani. Later, of course, Kreisler admitted he had written them himself."

In 1970 an LP record featuring Rosemary Brown, called "A Musical Séance," was pressed by Philips and released in the United States by Mercury. On one side are pieces played by Mrs. Brown herself, while on the other side more advanced pieces are played by concert pianist Peter Katin. Stewart Robb reviewed the record for *Psychic* magazine and commented on some of the critical shafts hurled at Rosemary and her music.

"Rosemary has studied piano for nearly four years but she is still an amateur, though with a pleasant enough touch," Robb observed.

The Katin side, however, is strikingly fine and some of the pieces he plays—he was given the more difficult ones which are obviously beyond Rosemary— are actually beginning to develop interesting careers.

Take for instance the Beethoven *Bagatelle,* which is now highly controversial. It is astonishing to read the diverse and contradictory comments on it, from believers and unbelievers alike. Amusingly, the disbelievers in its supra-mundane source are particularly

131

vulnerable as "authorities" for their opinions cancel one another out.

Irving Kolodin, for example, finds in it nothing of Beethoven, while Alan Rich of *New York* magazine hears in it passages from the *Appassionata*. Another critic suggests it was influenced by "Rage over a Lost Penny," while Leo Haber . . . in *The New York Times* . . . exclaims: "(This) work . . . alternates, runs and skips and chords and clearly recalls No. 23 of Beethoven's 33 Diabelli Variations."

Stewart Robb adds: "A musician, to whom I played this part of the record without telling him what it was, said reflectively, 'It sounds like a Beethoven *Bagatelle.*' "

Rosemary Brown has not received only music. Occasionally the composers communicate information about themselves.

Rosemary shared with me a bit of otherworldly gossip: Chopin and George Sand have long since broken up.

"They had very little in common spiritually," she told me gravely, "and besides, Chopin says he never did like a woman smoking cigars."

Once, when she was doing a program for the British Broadcasting Corporation, they inquired whether Liszt could give her some information about himself which was not readily available to the public but which could be checked in some way.

"Well, I asked Franz and he told me he had visited Leipzig in 1854 and while there was taken very ill," Rosemary recalled. "The BBC people said I must be wrong since Liszt stopped touring in 1848. But they had someone in Leipzig check.

"They found Liszt did visit there is 1854 and while there he fell ill with a bronchial cold and a serious ear infection."

Rosemary said that Brahms and Clara Schumann, the composer's wife, once appeared together. She had no idea, until someone told her, that Brahms had been a close friend of Mrs. Schumann.

The introduction to "A Musical Séance," Rosemary's record, is attributed to Sir Donald Tovey, a distinguished Scottish musicologist who died in 1940. This came about when David Hogarth, a staff writer with Philips Records in London, heard that Rosemary had been in touch with Sir Donald and suggested that he be asked to write an introductory note to the record. On New Year's Day, 1970, according to the medium, Tovey appeared and dictated what he wanted to say.

Hogarth, who long had been an admirer of Tovey's critical writing, did a careful analysis of the text on the basis of the musicologist's known literary style.

"As you listen to this record," the deceased Sir Donald said in his introduction, "you may wonder whether the music you hear is the product of Rosemary Brown's abilities or whether it has indeed emanated from departed composers who are still creating music in another world.

"The music itself already has called forth some admiration and denigration (as almost any music does) but I am happy to note that the former considerably outweighs the latter. I also note that those who denigrate the music usually do so not as a result of certain exacting standards but as the outcome of a measure of skepticism."

The Tovey introduction concluded: "In communicating through music and conversation, an organized group of musicians, who have departed from your world, are attempting to establish a precept for humanity—i.e., that physical death is a transition from one state of consciousness to another wherein one retains one's individuality. . . ."

In his analysis, David Hogarth allowed that he was struck by the likeness of the text to Tovey's actual writing style. He pointed out similarites in such matters as the use of humor, literary allusions, the proportion of words of Latin and Greek origin, and sentence construction.

Hogarth's summing up: "What conclusions can be drawn from this detailed examination? . . . I would be forced to accept the text as authentic Tovey if I had to judge it purely on its literary merits. Whether it is by Tovey or not, the piece is the product of a highly educated mind and a writer of no mean ability.

"With all due respect to Mrs. Brown I could not think for a moment that she had written it herself."

Tovey apparently considers Rosemary Brown his pupil. Once, when she was fumbling with a fugue Beethoven was trying to communicate, Tovey interrupted to say: "You can't understand this at all, can you?" He then proceeded to explain it to her while Beethoven stood by, presumably tapping his foot and trying to be patient with his less-than-brilliant amanuensis.

This incident led composer Richard Rodney Bennett to remark that he wished Tovey would help *him*.

One thoughful and perceptive student of the Rosemary Brown phenomenon, Sir George Trevelyan, warden of the Shropshire Adult College, has no doubts that her music proceeds from out-of-the-body sources.

"If we are to investigate it without prejudice," he said,

it is essential that we consider Rosemary's actual experience with an open mind as something new for which we can find no obvious explanation.

I sat with her at the piano and she described what was happening. "Chopin is here," she said. There was nothing eerie or spooky about the session. Chopin gave her a piece which she worked out phrase by phrase directly on the piano and in twenty minutes had it memorized and completed. Musicians will have some conception of what this feat involves.

There were moments when she even argued with him about notes or rendering.

Then Bach appeared. Here the approach was very different and she had to reach for score paper and set down complex phrases dictated note by note.

Then Beethoven came. She described him as completely recognizable but with something of a Greek look about him. He impresses music directly into her thinking in a manner which transcends our time sense, so that she has heard a symphony within ten minutes.

Trevelyan concludes: "The music will speak to those who are open for it and have goodwill towards the spirit, bringing the assurance that there is indeed continuity of consciousness beyond the gates of death and that fully conscious telepathic communion can now open possibilities of creative cooperation between those still on earth and those who have passed on."

The noted psychical researcher Dr. W. H. C. Tenhaeff, professor of parapsychology at the State University of Utrecht, analyzed the Rosemary Brown case from the standpoint of its credibility as evidence of communication from the dead.

"Although I most certainly do not reject the possibility that in Rosemary's case there is contact with the hereafter, I am of the opinion that we must not without

134

further consideration assume this is so," Dr. Tenhaeff said.

Then, in the style of a true scientist, he proceeded to weigh alternative explanations of the phenomenon.

One of the first questions a psychologist would ask about Rosemary Brown's case is whether it is not an example of what is called cryptomnesia—literally, hidden memory. Much more is stored in the human memory than we are conscious of and sometimes this unconsciously absorbed material is reproduced masquerading as messages from the dead.

"Flournoy, a French investigator, writes about a woman who had a reputation as a medium," Tenhaeff said.

One day she had a vision.

An Arab stepped towards her and held up a drawing. The woman took up a pencil and began to copy what she "saw" on a sheet of paper. On investigation it appeared that the characters were not only real Arabic characters but that they formed the words of an Arab proverb.

As it was known that the medium had never before occupied herself with Arabic, and had no knowledge of the language, it was supposed that this was a case of cryptomnesia and that at some time in the past she had been confronted with the text.

Inquiries showed that as a child she had been treated by a doctor who in his spare time had done Oriental studies. When Flournoy showed this doctor the Arab characters copied by the medium he cried, "It's as though I n looking at my own handwriting!"

He said that many years before he had journeyed through North Africa and written a travelogue about it. He had inscribed the presentation copies with Arab proverbs. The first proverb was the one written by the medium.

The obvious conclusion was that she had handled the presentation copies and that her eye had fallen on the inscription. This supposition gains credibility when we know that the medium's version contains two spelling mistakes which very probably were also made by the doctor who, in the days when he published his travelogue, did not have a perfect command of Arabic.

It is known that similar cases occur among writers and composers, Tenhaeff said, and sometimes give rise to suspicions of plagiarism. He quoted a Dutch composer, Max Tak, as saying that it would be an endless task to try to track down all the cases of unintentional plagiarism in music.

However, the cryptomnesia theory does not hold water in Rosemary Brown's case, argues Tenhaeff, for one thing because of the huge number of compositions. To produce more than five hundred pieces derived from unconscious recollection of other composers' works presupposes a memory storehouse of staggering proportions. It would make Rosemary Brown almost as much of a phenomenon as if she were genuinely receiving music from the dead.

Well, how do we know that Rosemary Brown isn't an astounding musical prodigy who creates her music out of a unique and unclassifiable genius? Maybe the "spirits" who appear to her and talk to her are merely phantasms of her own mind. Perhaps this is the way her idiosyncratic unconscious works—just as Tartini heard his dazzling *Devil's Sonata*, note for note, in a dream, and Coleridge received his poem "Kubla Khan" during an opium dream.

"If so," said Dr. Tenhaeff, "we can assume the apparitions of which she speaks to be products of a dramatized splitting of her personality. That they claim to be deceased composers can be accounted for by pointing out that the content of such apparitions is determined by the cultural environment of the person. Had Mrs. Brown lived in the Middle Ages she might have thought herself inspired by heavenly being which could have appeared to her, for instance, as seraphs."

But Tenhaeff contends that this explanation, persuasive as it is, will only fit Rosemary's case if the facts are distorted to fit the theory.

One of the most profound characteristics of the creative process, whether it be in creating music, literature, or visual art, is the "I" character of the product, Tenhaeff argues. The work bears the indelible imprint of the artist's ego, of his personality, of his own inimitable style. But in Rosemary Brown's case her compositions bear a distinctly "non-I" character. She feels, and has always felt, them to be the product of minds quite different and distinct from her own.

The spirit hypothesis is very tempting as an explanation of Rosemary Brown's music, Tenhaeff admits, but he cautions against jumping to this conclusion.

"Anyone with the necessary psychological training and versed in the study of paranormal phenomena knows what an extremely difficult field of research we are faced with here," he warns.

"I only feel justified in acknowledging that the Rosemary Brown case is an extremely interesting one. Thorough and continued study by a group of experts will, I trust, bring us closer to the solution of the problem posed by her compositions."

Some students of the Rosemary Brown phenomenon are persuaded that there are only two possible alternatives: Either she is indeed in communication with departed composers or some bizarre conspiracy to hoax the public must be assumed.

This view was expressed by Roy Douglas, a British musician, in *Psychic News*, Britain's largest Spiritualist weekly. Commenting on two of Rosemary's compositions, a Liszt-style piano piece and a piece of Brahms-style chamber music, he said:

"I consider it almost certainly impossible for her (Mrs. Brown) to have invented an imitation of these late works because: a. they are very rarely heard; b. few copies are in existence; c. comparatively few professional musicians would be sufficiently familiar with them to be able to compose imitations."

The skeptic faces a dilemma, argued Douglas. "If one is determined to account for her work in terms of the mundane, there are only two absurd theories I can think of:

1. A sealed parcel, arriving in her home now and then, containing manuscript from a very clever and dishonorable musician, with the message, 'Here's my latest imitation of . . .' together with a picture of the relevant deceased composer.

2. The same dishonorable musician, in Svengali-like cloak and mask, hypnotizing Mrs. Brown and dictating his fabrication to her in trance!

"Failing these fantasies, there seems to be only one explanation—the music is coming from the composers themselves."

However, I would say: Not necessarily. Maybe such an either-or dichotomy is too simplistic.

Before expressing my own views about how the Rosemary Brown phenomenon can be interpreted, let me say that I consider it one of the most curious, exciting, and significant psychic manifestations of our time.

Apart from her mediumship, I was impressed by Rosemary Brown as a person. She struck me as being sensitive, intelligent, kindly, sincere, and singularly down-to-earth in her attitude toward herself, without a trace of a Joan-of-Arc complex.

While I am incompetent to judge the merits of the music, it is obvious, from the comments of knowledgeable critics, that we have here something much more meaningful than the pathetic effusions of the typical middle-aged glandular case who thinks she is receiving communications from the seventh astral plane.

The material received by Mrs. Brown probably is among the most impressive in the history of mediumship. I liken it to the literary canon—more than 3 million words of novels, poems, prayers, and proverbs—produced through automatic writing in the 1920s by Mrs. Louise Curran of St. Louis, who left school at fourteen. That outpouring purportedly came from a sixteenth century Englishwoman named Patience Worth.

The nonmusical communications received by Rosemary Brown strike me as distinctly more plausible than those one gets from many mediums. More times than I care to reflect upon, I have sat in dim rooms listening to the platitudinous drivel, couched in pompous rhetoric, of some self-styled spirit guide. Rosemary Brown does not go in for platitudinous drivel.

Richard Rodney Bennett, a distinguished composer, tells her of a problem he is having with a Debussy prelude and he receives prompt and apt advice. A knowledgeable critic analyzes a text purportedly dictated by Sir Donald Tovey and finds it remarkably true to the famous musicologist's style. Liszt is asked to provide some obscure but verifiable information about himself and, without the waffling and evasiveness which the "spirits" so often exhibit, mentions a little-known illness in Leipzig in 1854.

And Debussy drops in for a chat with me and discusses a piece of his music in terms which, for me, were certainly understandable and meaningful.

Do I, then, believe that I was actually in communication with Monsieur Debussy?

That is a complex question. If only the matter of human survival after death were as simple as some believers say it is. Or as some unbelievers say it is. But, for me, it is much too subtle, many-faceted, and elusive an issue for instant certainties—one way or the other.

As Professor Tenhaeff intimated, because we have no satisfactory alternative explanation at hand we should not leap to the conclusion that the answer must be communication with the dead. It may simply be that other, more likely, explanations haven't yet occurred to us.

We should remember, for example, that nineteenth century Spiritualists were profoundly impressed by the often dramatic personality changes which mediums experienced in trance. The assumption was that such a striking phenomenon could only be explained by possession of the medium's body by a departed spirit. Nowadays, however, even a naive Spiritualist is more cautious.

In this Freudian age we understand more about human psychodynamics. We know that the human personality is capable, under some circumstances, of splitting into two or more subselves, and the spirits of the dead in these cases having nothing do with it. (The celebrated *Three Faces of Eve* described such a case of multiple personality.) When a medium's trance-personality manifests, the modern psychical researcher asks himself: Is this really the spirit of a dead person speaking or a secondary personality of the medium?

Mind you, there are still some cases of purported trance possession of the living by the dead which are hard to account for in conventional psychiatric terms, but this is beside the point as far as my present argument is concerned. I am simply pointing out that we are much less impressed today by the simple phenomenon of trance-speaking, as such, than people were a century ago.

It may be that future discoveries about the human mind will shed similar light on how a musically unsophisticated person such as Rosemary Brown could create marvelous music.

There may, in fact, be a clue in current research in the Soviet Union, about which Shiela Ostrander and Lynn Schroeder, authors of *Psychic Discoveries Behind the Iron Curtain*, told me. They described Soviet experiments in fostering human potential through a technique called "controlled reincarnation."

Actually, it has nothing to do with reincarnation. The Soviet researchers put a subject into a profound hypnotic trance that may last as long as several weeks and evoke a pseudo-personality possessing skills the subject normally does not have. A musician, for example, is told he is a celebrated painter. As he lives the hypnotic role, he actually develops unusual painting skill. Or a painter is told that he is a famous inventor, and obligingly masters mathematics.

When the subject is awakened from the "controlled reincarnation" experiment, say the Soviet researchers, the hypnotically evoked skills remain.

Could the huge, normally untapped potential of the human brain be the key to Rosemary Brown's amazing music?

And could the form in which the music comes to her, as dictation from dead composers, be the result of self-hypnosis or self-suggestion based on her Spiritualist beliefs?

If Mrs. Brown were a devout Roman Catholic, would she be receiving messages from one or several of the saints, or from the Virgin Mary? The question is not silly; millions of pilgrims annually visit the shrines at Lourdes and Fatima because of visionary communications to young women which, though different in content, are not essentially different in form, from the spirit visitations that Rosemary receives.

Or is it possible that Rosemary Brown somehow is psychically tapping the Jungian collective unconscious, that cosmic memory pool into which our individual deep minds feed, and which is said to contain the accumulated experiences of the race?

Some observers have mentioned that occasionally the medium's music is similar to one or several compositions in existence. Is it possible that she is picking up music from living minds, and from manuscripts, by extended telepathy and clairvoyance, a sort of super-ESP? If so, the ESP is fantastically selective. Nonetheless, it is a theoretical possibility which must be considered.

It may be that the music is derived from a variety of sources supernormally, some pieces being copies of existent compositions and others original creations of the medium's deep mind.

140

Of course, since nothing is too amazing to be true, as Faraday said, it is distinctly possible that Rosemary Brown is doing exactly what she says she's doing—having daily conversations with Beethoven, et al. The final judgment a person makes on this issue will not, I fancy, be based purely on the Rosemary Brown data. Probably it will arise largely from his broader views about the nature of personality and the plausibility of the idea of life after death in principle.

At any rate, Rosemary Brown, wherever your wonderful music comes from, keep it coming. . . .

NINE

Have You Died Before?
—An Interview with
Dr. Ian Stevenson

*The usual question is: What evidence
have we that somebody who died is still
alive? Now a brilliant scientist argues
that a better question may be: What evidence have we that somebody who lives
ever really died?*

DR. IAN STEVENSON, a prominent American psychiatrist—formerly chairman of the department of psychiatry
and neurology at the University of Virginia Medical
School—says there is persuasive evidence that some
human beings live more than one life on this earth.

Evidence, mind you, not *proof*.

Stevenson's scientifically cautious approach is reflected
in the title of his book, *Twenty Cases Suggestive of Reincarnation* (New York, the American Society for Psychical
Research, 1966). In it, the Montreal-born researcher, who
is listed in the prestigious *American Men of Science*, describes instances of apparent rebirth which he has personally investigated.

The cases cited are from countries as diverse as India
and Ceylon (where the Hindu and Buddhist majorities accept reincarnation as a religious doctrine) to Brazil,
Lebanon, and the United States. In most instances the
central figure in the case is a child who appears to have
memories—and sometimes other psychological, and even
physical, characteristics—pertaining to a previous life on
earth.

One case is that of a boy in India named Ravi Shankar
(no relation to the famed concert star). When he was
between the ages of two and three he began to claim
that he had lived before as a boy named Munna. He "re-

membered" his home in a city some two hundred miles from the backward village where he was then living.

He said he could recall the circumstances of his death, and he often talked about them. He insisted that he had been stabbed at the age of six by two ruffians.

When Ravi Shankar was four years old, he met the father of Munna, the murdered boy. He was able to describe in detail many incidents in the life of Munna, the house where he had lived, his toys, other members of the family, and his demise.

Ravi Shankar pointed to a birthmark on his throat which resembled the scar of a knife wound. He insisted that it was a carry-over from his murder in his previous life; that he, as Munna, had been stabbed in the throat. The detail was correct.

The father of Munna was convinced that Ravi Shankar was indeed his deceased son reborn in another body.

Dr. Stevenson made an intensive on-the-spot investigation of the case in 1964, using not only the standard methods of a good reporter but his special skills as a psychiatrist in evaluating the credibility of witnesses and ferreting out motives for posible conscious or unconscious distortion, or fraud. His conclusion: Ravi Shankar did possess intimate knowledge of the life of the late Munna and it is exceedingly unlikely that he could have learned this by normal means.

As was true in this case, the people with purported memories of a previous life sometimes bear idiosyncratic birthmarks which appear to relate to the former incarnation. One of the most impressive cases which Stevenson has studied is that of Corliss Chotkin, Jr.

Chotkin is part Tlingit Indian, part Anglo-Saxon, now in his early twenties, and lives in Alaska. The Tlingits are the Alaskan aborigines and reincarnation is a part of their folklore that remains very much alive in the minds of many members of the tribe.

In 1946 a full-blooded Tlingit named Victor Vincent said to his niece: "I'm coming back after I die, as your son. Your son will have these scars." He pointed to a scar on the right side of his nose, under his eye, and to one on his back. Both were the result of surgery.

Shortly after making his prediction—not all that strange among the Tlingits, who believe that a person can choose his next parents—Victor Vincent died. About eighteen months later his niece bore a son, named Corliss Chotkin, Jr.

The boy had two odd birthmarks. One was on the right side of his nose, just below the eye, although as the child grew it moved downward with the elongation of the tissues. The other scar was on his back. These were recognized by the parents and others who had known Victor Vincent as being identical to the surgical scars he had borne.

When the boy was thirteen months old, his parents reported, he suddenly said: "Don't you know me? I'm Kahkody." This was the Tlingit tribal name of the deceased Victor Vincent.

As he grew, the boy is said to have muttered from time to time: "I'm Victor. Don't you remember my promise?"

Young Corliss recounted incidents from the life of Victor Vincent which often were unknown to his parents, but which were verified by intimates of the deceased. For example, the boy said that once he, as Victor, had been out in his fishing boat when he ran out of gas; he recalled getting help by putting on his Salvation Army uniform, which he always carried with him apparently (Victor was an ardent Salvationist), and flagging down a passing steamship, the *North Star*. This incident was verified.

The boy developed many personality traits, it was said, which were strikingly similar to the dead man's and unlike his parents'.

For one thing, young Corliss, alone among the members of his family, developed a fondness for the Salvation Army and loved Gospel hymns. For another, he talked with a stammer, again the only member of his family to do so; Victor Vincent had a lifelong stammer.

Also, the boy showed a pronounced aptitude for tinkering with engines, something the dead man always enjoyed. The boy's parents cited what they considered another similarity: Corliss moved with an odd shuffling gait which reminded them of Victor Vincent's way of walking.

Ian Stevenson made three extended trips to Alaska to study the Corliss Chotkin case. He scrutinized and photographed the boy's birthmarks and concluded that they dramatically resembled surgical scars. In the one on the back, he noted, stitch marks were plainly visible.

Dr. Stevenson cross-examined a large number of witnesses and concluded that fraud or sheer error could not account for many of the strange parallels between Corliss Chotkin, Jr., and his deceased great-uncle Victor Vincent.

Dr. Stevenson summed up the evidence for reincarnation in this case "Since the marks on Corliss Chotkin's body were definitely congential and not hereditary, they can have had only one of two origins: Either they arose from some intrauterine influence or from some other influence put into play before conception.

"But we cannot conceive of any intrauterine accident during gestation which would cause a birthmark resembling the scar of a surgical wound with stitch marks. . . . I would think these marks evidence that the influence which caused them on the embryonic body of Corliss Chotkin came from the deceased mind of Victor Vincent."

The boy's detailed knowledge of Victor's life, said Stevenson, indicated "that somehow he had access to the mind of Victor Vincent; that is, that Victor's personality was reincarnated in and was continuous with that of Corliss Chotkin, Jr."

Another case in which physical stigmata, if you like, appear to derive from a previous life is that of Wijeratne Hami in Ceylon.

This young man, now in his twenties, was born with a badly deformed right arm. When he was two years old, his mother heard him muttering around the house about his arm's being crippled because he had murdered his wife in his past incarnation, and the law of karma (the moral law of cause and effect, from one earthly life to the next, in which Buddhists and Hindus believe) was working its justice.

The mother told her husband. He was disturbed. Both the man and his wife had remarked before upon certain startling resemblances between their young son and the man's dead brother. In fact, the father had said: "This is my brother come back."

That thought reopened a very painful memory. The father of Wijeratne, whose name was H. A. Tileratne Hami, had had a brother, some fifteen years younger, called Ratram. On October 14, 1927, Ratram got into an altercation with his young wife, Podi Menike, over her refusal to leave her parents' home and return with him to his village. Ratram apparently drew a knife and fatally stabbed her.

He was tried, convicted, and sentenced to hang. Before he was executed, in July, 1928, he said to his brother:

"I am not afraid. I know I must die. I am only worried about you. Don't sorrow, my brother. I will return."

In August, 1961, Ian Stevenson personally investigated the alleged rebirth of Ratram Hami as Wijeratne, his brother's son.

The boy, who was then fourteen, told Stevenson that he definitely remembered the gallows, and the sensations he had experienced as the trap was sprung. He felt as though he were plunging into a pit of fire, he said; then he recalled nothing until he was two years old and realized that he had been reborn as his brother's child.

Wijeratne's mother attested that the boy had described many details surrounding the killing of Podi Menike, including the reasons for the domestic squabble leading up to it, of which the mother at the time was unaware, but which her husband and others were able later to verify. There seemed to be no normal way in which a very young child could have known these facts.

In his careful, characteristically detailed summary of the case of Wijeratne, Stevenson argues that there is evidence of some form of "paranormal" knowledge about the deceased Ratram by the boy. With due caution, he opts for the reincarnation hypothesis as the one which most adequately covers all the facts in the case.

Another case in which there was an apparent rebirth of a previous personality within the same family, but in a culture unsympathetic to the idea of reincarnation, is that of Paulo Lorenz of Brazil. In this case, there are also elements of behavioral and psychological characteristics apparently linked to the former life.

On October 12, 1921, nineteen-year-old Emilia Lorenz died from a self-administered dose of cyanide. There had been several previous suicide attempts.

During her short life, Emilia had often spoken of her dislike of being a woman. She said, her brothers and sisters recalled, that if there were such a thing as reincarnation she wanted to come back as a man.

However, Emilia, despite her lack of enthusiasm about being female, showed what appears to have been a remarkable skill—Ian Stevenson calls it "almost genius"—at sewing, although no other member of the family, including her mother, shared this ability.

Shortly after Emilia's death her mother attended several spiritualistic séances where she received messages, purportedly from the dead girl, saying that she wanted to rejoin the family circle as a boy.

Mrs. Lorenz told her husband about these communications and both claimed that they expressed distinct disapproval of the idea of a masculinized Emilia. Besides, they had twelve children and another one was out of the question.

However, on February 3, 1923, less than two years after Emilia's death, Mrs. Lorenz had a son. His parents named him Emilio but his familiar nickname always was Paulo.

Up to the age of five, Paulo refused to wear boy's clothes, insisting on dressing as a girl. He showed an innate flair for sewing, apparently to quite an unusual extent, and this was remarked upon by his parents and siblings.

Finally, when he was five, Paulo agreed to wear a pair of trousers made from an old skirt of Emilia's. From that time on he became more masculine in his orientation and his enthusiasm for sewing faded. However, into adulthood, his masculinity remained far below the norm.

In 1962, when Ian Stevenson personally investigated Paulo's case, he had not married, though he was thirty-nine; he had virtually no contact with women except his sisters; and he scored very low in masculinity on a psychological projection test which Stevenson administered.

In assessing this case as evidence of reincarnation, the researcher notes that, since the present and previous personalities were both in the same family, the task of ruling out normal communication of information about the former personality becomes more difficult. Also, it is possible to argue that Paulo's marked sewing skill, which he alone among his siblings shared with the dead Emilia, might have been hereditary. Stevenson notes too, however, that this would not explain why only Paulo inherited the ability. Nor is the idea of heredity strengthened by the fact that Mrs. Lorenz herself showed a conspicuous lack of sewing ability.

Another case studied by Ian Stevenson suggests that curious predilections—in this instance, for a name—may be linked to unconscious memories of a previous life.

A Dutch portrait painter, who now lives in New York, was born Henriette Roos. She married a man called Weisz whom she subsequently divorced. Although in Holland it is the custom for women to resume their maiden names after a divorce, Mrs. Weisz, for some unaccountable reason, liked her married name and did not want to give it up. "Somehow that name suits me," she said when her mother reproved her for not resuming her maiden one, "somehow it is more me than my own name."

As a compromise, she decided to call herself Mrs. Weisz-Roos.

She went to Paris to paint and worked very hard to support herself. One night, tossing fitfully, she heard an audible voice say: "Don't be so lazy. Get up and work."

She opened her eyes cautiously. She was alone, as she had known she was. She got up, went to her easel, and, impressed to paint in the dark, did so in a feverish haste, hardly knowing what she was doing. After a while she felt very sleepy and returned to bed. The next morning she found she had painted a beautiful mini-portrait of a young woman.

Puzzled by the experience, Mrs. Weisz-Roos described it to a friend who advised her to consult a clairvoyant. The psychic touched the portrait she had painted and then went into a trance.

"Letters," he murmured in a hoarse voice, "I see very large golden letters. And a name. . . . It is G-O-Y-A. Goya, the great Spanish painter.

"He tells me that he was forced to fly from his country because of his enemies. It was you who received him in your home; it was you who offered him protection in your home in a big southern city in France. He lived with you until the end of his life.

"Goya has remained so thankful for your kindness in that life that he wishes to guide you. You seldom relax your guard. You make it most difficult for him to repay his debt. That was why he made you paint in the dark, so you could not see what you were doing."

At the time of the séance, Mrs. Weisz-Roos had never read anything about Goya. That same evening, however, she looked up a biography of the painter and was astonished to find in it an account of a woman in whose home Goya had lived during his exile from Spain at the end of his life. Her name: Leocadia Weisz.

Needless to say, theories other than reincarnation have been proposed to explain the sort of cases reported by Ian Stevenson. Generally these fall into two main categories: conventional, or nonpsychic, and paranormal.

Among the first are fraud, cryptomnesia (hidden or buried memories), and so-called genetic memory (inherited recollections imprinted somehow on the germ plasm).

In the second group, the favorite theory appears to involve a combination of super-ESP and the fantasizing and dramatizing powers of the unconscious, which, so the theory goes, can produce the verisimilitude of a playback of a previous life. The leading exponent of this interpretation of Stevenson's data is Professor C. T. K. Chari of Madras Christian College, India. (See his "Paramnesia and Reincarnation" in the *Proceedings* of the Society for Psychical Research, Volume 53, Part 193, December, 1962.)

In a long interview with Ian Stevenson, who was a guest in my home, I asked him about these alternative theories and many other subjects, during a wide-ranging discussion of his research and the insights he had distilled out of it. Here is a transcript of our tape-recorded conversation that took place in January, 1968.

ALLEN SPRAGGETT: How did your reincarnation research begin?

IAN STEVENSON: It was about fifteen years ago, I guess, when I first began to read sporadic reports of cases of apparent rebirth. These were published in the literature in single case reports or occasionally in groups of five or six. I began to put them into a notebook, sorting them out into different countries, and after I had done that for about five years, I realized that there really were quite a few of them.

Then I wrote my first article, "The Evidence for Survival from Claimed Memories of Former Incarnations," using forty-four cases that had already been published. (This appeared in the *Journal of the American Society for Psychical Research*, April and July, 1960, and won the William James Prize.)

A. S.: Were you attracted to reincarnation for its own sake, so to speak, or, as you suggested in your William James essay, because it offered the most fruitful way of proving human survival after death?

I. S.: Well, both. It's very hard to reconstruct just what the influential factors were that pushed me into it. But certainly one was the thought that here, if the reincarnation cases were authentic, was some rather strong evidence of survival—and it might be a new line of inquiry into the survival question which, as you know, almost thirty years ago got sort of stuck with the withdrawal of most parapsychologists into laboratory card-guessing experiments. There was a virtual arrest of interest in the survival question. In fact, when I started my rebirth investigations, there were then, and still are, only three parapsychologists in the world who were seriously interested in survival: Myself; Karlos Osis of the American Society for Psychical Research, who did a superb study of deathbed visions; and William Roll of Durham, North Carolina, who works with mediums.

A. S.: Were you a parapsychologist when you started your reincarnation research?

I. S.: Technically, no; I was just an orthodox professor. But the other reason for my getting into rebirth research was my dissatisfaction with conventional theories of personality, based on heredity and childhood environment. I sensed that there was something very deficient in the Freudian theories. Before I got into parapsychology I wrote a number of papers criticizing common psychiatric myths. I was well aware even then of the limitations of these other theories.

A. S.: What sort of limitations?

I. S.: The Freudian theories of twenty or thirty years ago emphasized that you were born, and you might have a little bit of heredity in there—they weren't paying much attention even to heredity, although Freud acknowledged its importance—but in effect you were just like plasticine in the hands of your parents. You were shaped up by them. And everything that happened to you in the first year was critical, and then the second year was almost as critical but not quite, the third year was very important, the fourth year too and the fifth, and by the sixth year, that was it. You were a finished product. Then you were supposed to go on into your so-called latent period.

Well, there were a lot of cases that just did not fit, didn't fit at all.

A. S.: Did you believe at that time that mind and brain were different?

I. S.: Yes, I think I believed this virtually all my life—that mind was different from brain. The theory that mind is brain is not even supported by studies of perception. There are serious defects in explaining ordinary,

151

normal perception on that basis.

Anyway, about a year after the William James essay I got an initial small grant to go to India and study a rebirth case that had come up. On that trip, I also studied some other cases, about twenty in India and three or four in Ceylon.

Then, not too long after that, I got more money which enabled me to give up private practice; up to that point I'd had to earn a good deal of my salary by seeing private patients. Then the donor, a few years later, endowed a chair for me, and I was able to give up the chairmanship of the department of psychiatry and neurology and devote myself more or less full time to parapsychology. Now my title is Alumni Professor of Psychiatry.

A. S.: How many rebirth cases have you collected?

I. S.: About a thousand on the books. Of these I must have investigated some six hundred. And, of these, I've had interviews with, say three hundred.

A. S.: What's the collapse rate among the cases you get to study fairly closely? How many turn out to be obvious fantasy or fraud?

I. S.: The collapse rate among the cases you get around to is very low—fewer than 5 percent. Although I think I would have to differentiate between the American and the Asian cases.

The Asian cases do have a very low collapse rate; they stand up well under careful examination. Usually extravagant claims don't enter into these cases. The children claim to have been some other peasant in their previous life, rarely a wealthy person and very rarely some prominent person.

Now, there are some cases of this sort in America, too, but they are generally much less detailed and therefore less convincing. In America, in addition to the children's cases, we also get sort of adult fantasy cases. These often feature prominent historical personalities whom the adult claims to be, reborn. "Stevenson's rule" says, the more prominent the claimed previous personality, the weaker the evidence.

But in all the cases there is very little outright fraud. There was one I can think of in India of a child who was claiming to be Mahatma Gandhi reborn, complete with birthmarks. The boy was caught boning up on information about Gandhi and there seems little doubt it's a fraud case.

There were, in this case, features that were atypical to begin with. For example, the boy didn't start talking about the previous life until he was nine, and that is suspicious because nearly all the genuine cases start with the child remembering from the ages of two to five, almost as soon as he can speak. If the child doesn't start talking about it until he's nine, that's suspicious.

A. S.: How many of the rebirth cases

involve pretty clear mental illness?

I. S.: Very few. Most of these children—and I've followed a number of them, and am in touch with some who were cases when they were young and are now adults—have grown up into just ordinary people.

Now, they may be modified to some extent by the previous experiences, and there may be residues of the previous life, if you like, in their personality. But in other respects they have developed entirely normally and become professional people— teachers, lawyers, professors— and peasants. Just ordinary people, most of them.

A. S.: There are many different kinds of alleged reincarnation cases reported—spontaneous memories in children, hypnotic regression à la Bridey Murphy, birthmarks. What is the most evidential kind of case?

I. S.: By far the best are the spontaneous recall cases in children. I think the hypnotic regression cases are awfully feeble. What you get, really, with hypnosis, is a kind of dream state—and the imagination can run free. You may get an historical novel, actually—elements of perhaps a previous life obtruding, and then a big layer of fantasy on top of that.

In a few cases, where there was conscious recall, I've used hypnosis to try to amplify the recall. But there again, the hypnotic state, unless it's carefully controlled, may simply

154

amplify the expectations of the subject from the preliminary memories.

I don't want to reject hypnotic regression altogether because I think it does have value. But to take these cases at face value is a great mistake.

A. S.: How might you control the hypnotic regression to reduce the fantasy?

I. S.: One way would be to regress children, between the ages of, say, eight and fifteen. You have more control over what they've read and what they might know, and they wouldn't be so likely as adults to have expectations. I'm planning to do some of these when I get the time. Actually, I tried one with a boy of fifteen, but he wasn't a very good hypnotic subject, unlike most children, and I got nothing.

A. S.: The strongest evidence, then, is provided by spontaneous memories in children? Do birthmarks strengthen such cases?

I. S.: Yes. Some of my new cases with birthmarks, which come from a small Islamic sect in the south of Turkey, are the best evidence yet, I think.

The frequency of birthmarks, however, depends on the culture. They come up much more in some cultures than others. I think this is mainly because of the style of death. The birthmarks are particularly associated with neat, clean wounds from bullets, spears, and knives. And you don't get them so much in a technological culture where a person is just pulped in an automobile accident. Or if he dies a natural death.

Of course, the birthmarks aren't always associated with violent wounds. They can derive from surgical scars, as the case of Corliss Chotkin. This, by the way, is one of the strongest cases from the standpoint of evidence.

One of the criticisms about the birthmark cases has been that, well, everybody has birthmarks of one kind or another. But, in the first place, in most of these cases, we're not concerned with appearances like ordinary moles, although moles do enter into it occasionally. Most of these birthmarks actually look like healed wounds that have been acquired. They are, to me, indistinguishable. In many cases they are just like a scar. Often they have three-dimensional properties, although some of them are just pigmented changes.

But a lot of them actually are pitted or puckered and look just like a scar, an acquired wound.

Now, one might say that, well, these just happened to occur, and it's difficult to be certain that there really is a noncoincidental correspondence between the mark on the subject and the mark on the deceased personality.

Okay, but when you have two birthmarks in specific locations, as in the Corliss Chotkin case, and these are then related to two wounds on the previous personality, the evidence becomes much stronger. Because the likelihood of two marks on one body, in different locations, corresponding to two marks on another body in the same locations, is a very improbable one.

Well, in the Corliss Chotkin case, as I say, you have that. There was a mark on the nose and a mark on the back. For the one on the back I never could get medical documentation, but there is the testimony of the boy's parents and others who knew the deceased Victor Vincent that he did indeed have such a scar. On the boy, the mark on the back was extraordinary—stich marks were plainly visible, although these have faded somewhat with age.

For the other mark on Victor Vincent, I got medical documentation; it was the result of an eye operation, just under his right eye, and left the appropriate scar for the nose birthmark. The birthmark on the boy was originally under the eye, but it drifted down as Corliss grew. That's another authenticating feature, actually, that some of these birthmarks move. On the newborn baby, the scar was just under the eye, but as the tissues elongated—for the head changes in relation to the body as the child grows—then the scar moved down and ended up near the base of his nose.

Other birthmarks I've studied appear like the scars of healed knife wounds, of bullet wounds, and so on.

A. S.: What is the mechanism that imprints the scar on the present body?

I. S.: Obviously I don't have the answer to this, although I think about it a great deal.

Buddhism has an answer. Buddhism says it is the intensity of carving that does the imprinting. It's the desire for the body or for the possessions that a person is leaving. All this leads to heightened emotion and this appears to be crucial to the imprinting. There is one case, published by my friend Francis Story, that illustrates rather neatly the Buddist point of view.

This was the case of a Karen houseboy—the Karens are a sort of Burmese minority group —whom my friend had working for him in Rangoon. The boy had odd deformities. He had deep grooves in the palms of both his hands and in some of his fingers—real crevasses. He had similar grooves on his calves. And he had a couple of toes glued together, as it were, on his left foot. As I recall, the right arm was particularly badly affected.

This boy was about twenty when my friend knew him. His story was that he remembered his previous life. He said he had been a moderately wealthy person who had become a widower and was much sought after by eligible women. But he was married to his money.

He was very avaricious, a

miser in fact, and he kept his money in jars hidden around the house. Eventually he became so notoriously wealthy and avaricious that robbers decided he was ripe for the plucking.

So they came and tied him up in a sort of bundle, in a squatting position. They tied his hands with wire and wound the wire so tightly that it cut into his hands and into his thighs as he squatted on the floor, and some blood dripped down on to the toes of his left foot. Leaving him in this position, the robbers ransacked the house.

The miser stayed there for a number of days and then, after a while, he became aware of a body that seemed to be in a strangely crouched position in one corner of the room. He became aware that it was his late physical body, and that he was separated from his body, was out of it. He was dead. And, the next thing, he came to as his mother's child, reborn.

The Karen houseboy had all the deformities related to his having been bound with wire, and he remembered his death. Interestingly enough, when he talked about it he used to have a painful swelling of his arm, very much the way it is when people abreact something of this life. They may have a reopening of wounds, if they've been beaten as children, you know. And he had this, except that it went back to the previous life.

Now the Buddhist theory

would say that if the miser hadn't been so greedy, he wouldn't have hung around the body and his pots of gold; if he had been a more developed person, he wouldn't have had this craving for terrestrial possessions. It was this emotion, the avarice, which kept him stuck there, hovering near the dead body, and which led to the imprinting of the death marks on the next body. Otherwise, if he had just yielded up his body and gone about his business in the next world, things would have been much better for him.

A. S.: Is the transmission of scars from one life to the next analogous to hysterical lesions reproduced on the body by mental states in this life? For instance, the stigmatist reproduces on his own body the traditional wounds of Christ by an intense identification with the image of the crucified savior.

I. S.: Yes, I think it is a good analogy. Certainly the emotional component is very important in these birthmark cases. Immediately, of course, you get into a dualist view of man here, because you are supposing some entity, some structure, which carries over the imprint of the marks from one life to the next.

One reason why I was very interested in the psychic photography of Ted Serios was that he seemed to be doing to photographic film what my subjects were doing to embryos with their birthmarks. And indeed, if

Serios had remained in a positive phase, I had intended to see if he could influence bacterial colonies.

I was going to hold agar plates with bacteria on them and discover if he could mark them. You see, if you paint a plate of bacteria with a solution of penicillin, say, and you paint "P" on the bacteria, they die in the shape of the "P" and you get a sort of death ray effect. Well, it seemed to me that if Serios could activate photographic film he might be able to activate sensitive microorganisms like bacteria and I wanted to see if he could develop an imprint on a bacterial colony. That would have been a closer link to biological phenomena such as you get in the birthmarks.

There are a few anomalous cases where the birthmark must have appeared in the late stages of the fetus. In certain cases I have, the death of the murderee whose wounds are going to be reproduced on the baby may occur—as reported—a very few days before the birth of the baby. And yet the wound is there when the baby is born. So it is as if there's an instant reproduction of the wound.

A. S.: You mean, in such cases, the baby has been in the womb almost nine months, and then a personality who died just a few days before the baby's birth seems to have taken over the fetal body?

I. S.: Yes. In these cases one has to

161

suppose either that during pregnancy you just get a kind of physical organism waiting for a driver, the way you have an automobile delivered to a dealer, and the entity doesn't enter the body until just before birth. Or the other possibility is that there was an occupant, a builder of the body who was trying to shape it up to his own uses, and he was jostled aside by another entity which took over the body.

A. S.: How many of your rebirth cases remember the post-mortem period between earth incarnations?

I. S.: Amnesia for the intermission, as I call it, is fairly typical. Although quite a number of Thais remember it. And also a young girl in Ceylon had a lot to say about the intermission period, and it made considerable sense. What she and others have said accords with certain of the statements given out by Western mediums, and out-of-the-body travelers—that the next world is a world of images, of telepathic communication, with a different sense of time.

Why do some remember the intermission while others don't? Buddhism says it is recalled by some because they practised meditation and attained a higher level of consciousness before death, and their consciousness then is continuous after death. There is also the expectation and the hope of remembering, which probably intensifies the ability to remember.

A. S.: Do any of the cases talk about a vision of the Divine Being during the intermission?

I. S.: Well, a number refer to sadhus, sages, mahatmas, whom they claim to have met in the intermediate state, just as Catholics would meet saints, presumably.

The French Spiritualists talk of these people as *seignors de karma*—people who are roughly like a ticket agent at an airport, who tears off the ticket for your next flight and registers you in. There are some interesting reports of this sort of thing where, after a sojourn on the next plane, one is escorted down to one's next body by these people or their deputies.

A. S.: Is there evidence that people choose their next incarnation?

I. S.: You don't get that very much in Asia, but, curiously enough, you do in the Tlingit cases of Alaska. I've got ten Tlingit cases now where, before death, the person who was going to die made a selection of parents for the next incarnation.

In Buddhism you get less emphasis on willpower than you do among the Tlingits and more on earning through meritorious deeds. Maybe the Tlingits have been to some extent influenced by American meliorism—the feeling, you know, that anything is possible and that you can change things. Whereas in Asia there is more fatalism, even among Buddhists and Hindus, although of course in its more extreme form you get the fatalism of the Muslims with their doctrine of kismet (fate).

Be that as it may, the Tlingits do have, much more than any other group I've encountered, this idea that you can choose your own parents and they seem to have provided some evidence of having done this.

A. S.: Does the knowledge that one's deformity stems from a demerit in a previous life make it easier to adjust to it?

I. S.: Well, let's take the Ceylonese case of Wijeratne. He is, to begin with, the only case of mine where the deformity is on the murderer. In all other cases the deformity is on the murderee. So he is a very unusual case from that point of view, and I don't know the answer to that.

He made a prediction about coming back as his brother's son before he was hanged for the stabbing death of his wife. He is one of the unusual agents in Asia who apparently did set up his own parents.

It is hard to know whether he had remorse about his crime or not. When I saw him first, in 1961, he was about fourteen years old and at that time I raised the question with him of what he would do if he got married in a few years and his wife refused to go back to his village with him, as his wife in the previous life had refused. And he said, "Oh, I would kill her."

That showed little evidence of reform and I went away sad-

dened. Then I returned to see
him in 1966 and he spontaneously said that he had been thinking
the matter over and had
changed his mind, and that he
would not kill his wife if she
refused to accompany him back
to his village. He reaffirmed
that when I saw him again in
1968.

A. S.: Wijeratne appears to have interpreted the deformity of his
arm as the result of his having
used it to stab his wife to
death. . . . Do you find the idea
of a law of karma useful?

I. S.: I prefer not to talk about the
law of karma because that almost assumes certain theo-
sophical doctrines, and a lot of
them are based on fantasy.

However, it's not a bad word,
really. Karma literally means
action. It means the effect in one
life of causes generated in another.

Karma, of course, is not all
negative. In fact, the evidence
that points to reincarnation provides a basis for hope as well
as fear, whereas most modern
doctrines of psychology are
pretty hopeless—you are what
you are and there's little you
can do about it. With reincarnation there is a chance of later
remedies. It is the possibility of
another chance. And I think
that for many people this is an
incentive to moral reform.

A. S.: Are all physical deformities
karmic?

I. S.: There is so little evidence on
that. All one can say is that, if
any is, then possibly all are.

And if we have some cases in which missing arms, ears, fingers and so on seem to be related to these birthmarks, then it's at least provisionally conceivable that all deformities have some such explanation. But I wouldn't want to go that far now.

Some of the birthmarks appear hard to account for on a medical basis. Consider the peculiar grooves in the hands and thighs of the Karen houseboy. These seem to be unthinkable as any sort of intrauterine defect. Occasionally deformities are attributed to the umbilical cord getting wound around the fetus but this is most improbable as an explanation for this case.

I have a case in which a missing hand and a deformed foot appear to be karmic. The man apparently had been blown up by a shell in World War One on his last time around.

I'm very interested in studying cases where the effects of the injury in the previous life penetrated more deeply into the inner organs. Internal birthmarks, as it were.

In one case in Brazil involving a girl named Martha, the previous personality in effect committed suicide, after her father thwarted her, by standing in the rain and cold weather and developing a cold that turned into tuberculosis of the larynx. At the end of her life, just before she died, the previous personality lost her voice. She was practically aphonic and could just whisper very slightly.

So the apparently reborn Martha, as a young child, was susceptible to attacks of laryngitis, when she would lose her voice and become extremely hoarse. It was a kind of birthmark in the form of susceptibility to a particular disease.

In another case, eczema was related to a child having been burnt to death in a fire. The apparently reborn child had a tremendously red skin, as if *he* had been burnt, and then this gradually subsided.

I have currently about twenty cases with medical features. They seem to me very exciting because modern medicine has no answer for why X gets a particular disease.

There's Joe; he's found to have mitral stenosis, or cirrhosis of the liver, or cancer. And if you say, well why does Joe have cirrhosis of the liver, and Bill stomach cancer, they say, well, that's just the way things are. Here, through reincarnation, is the possibility of some insight into disease etiology that we haven't had before.

A. S.: Have you gleaned any insights into the ultimate meaning of human life from your reincarnation research?

I. S.: The ultimate purpose may be the realization of thoughts in the mind of God. Maybe we are being created, and creating ourselves, in the way an artist creates a painting. The purpose is creation, and creation in ever

167

richer and more complicated forms.

Things, perhaps, continue to go on evolving until there is a devolution to nothing again and then another cycle begins. I rather believe with the Buddhists on this point. They believe that the universe evolves and devolves and then, after a rest period, evolves again.

Each evolving universe, presumably, is better than the previous one in some respect or other, or at any rate different. So that after a period of quiescence lasting, say, a quarter-eternity, if you like, there is a new universe, and the new universe is an improvement, and God could imagine something better.

A. S.: The physical universe, then, is the "dream of Brahman," as the Hindus say, or the thought of God?

I. S.: Yes, I think so. . . .

What about alternative theories to reincarnation as explanations of the sort of data studied by Ian Stevenson?

In a number of instances, he has considered what he feels are the main alternatives and rejected them. In brief, the theories and their weaknesses, as Stevenson sees them, are as follows.

Ian Stevenson rejects fraud as a plausible explanation of most of his cases because, for one thing, what could be the motive?

Wealth? There is no evidence that anybody made any money in these cases, he says.

Notoriety? Most people in the cases have found any publicity that resulted "vexatious," Stevenson maintains. And such favorable publicity as has occurred has never seemed sufficient, to him, to compensate for the effort required in staging an elaborate hoax.

What about the argument that the hoax might satisfy a

psychological need? A child in a poor home, for example, could derive emotional satisfaction from claiming to have been the son of a wealthy family in his previous life.

True, says Stevenson. But in many cases the child is in a well-to-do home and remembers a life in a very poor family.

Besides, he points out, this psychological argument does not deal with the question of how these children came to possess intimate information about the previous personality, which appears not to have been accessible by normal means.

Moreover, most of these cases, if they were hoaxes, would have to be conspiracies involving several people, and sometimes a very large number indeed, for the child's claims often are reinforced or attested to by other members of the family or friends.

For reasons such as these, Stevenson concludes that the complexity of the cases makes fraud "virtually out of the question" as an explanation for most of them.

Another normal hypothesis, as opposed to a paranormal one, is cryptomnesia—literally, "hidden memory."

According to this theory, the child actually acquired the information he possessed about the previous personality by normal means, but forgot the source. Later, when he "remembered" his former life he was really uncovering these buried or hidden memories.

Stevenson argues that cryptomnesia, though more plausible than fraud, cannot account for all the data.

To cite just one example, in the Corliss Chotkin case, the boy, while still very young, mentioned incidents from the life of the deceased Victor Vincent which even his parents didn't know about, but which were found to be accurate. In such instances, where did so young a child acquire the information?

Further, argues Stevenson, cryptomnesia is not a very convincing explanation for what happened in some cases when a child was taken to the scene of his "remembered" former life, for the first time, and correctly identified objects which had belonged to the previous personality, members of the family, and so on.

Moreover, even if cryptomnesia were plausible as an explanation for most of the informational features of the cases, it does not cover the even more significant behavioral aspects. The duplication of the previous personality's peculiar walk, a stammer, predilection for sewing, and of course idiosyncratic physical marks—these, contends Stevenson, make cryptomnesia untenable.

Another suggested explanation of the rebirth cases is "genetic memory."

Stevenson commented: "Genetic memory is a far-out concept anyway, for most biologists. But it is definitely ruled out in most of my cases, simply because the two personalities are not genetically related. There's no lineal descent.

"Genetic memory may conceivably apply to cases where there are two or three hundred years between the A and B personalities and B is, or might be, a descendant of A. But it couldn't apply to cases where you have a short intermission between the lives, and two families totally unrelated, with no descent of one from the other."

The most persuasive alternative theory to reincarnation in the cases Stevenson cites seems to be what he calls "personation" and extrasensory perception. By personation he means the ability of the unconscious mind to impersonate another personality.

This theory contends that the children in the rebirth cases pick up the information about the previous personality by a sort of extended ESP, and their unconscious then dramatizes these impressions into an apparent recollection of a previous life.

Stevenson carefully considers this theory, recognizing its force. He finds it less plausible than reincarnation on several grounds:

One is that ESP, from the experimental evidence, is typically inconstant; it comes in flashes. Rarely, if ever, does it function continuously, as does the "recall" these children have of their previous life.

Further, clairvoyant impressions do not normally take the form of reincarnational memories. Why, then, do they in these cases? The child usually insists that the impressions are indistinguishable from memories of events in his present life.

Again, too, Stevenson feels that ESP, however extended, cannot plausibly account for the behavioral features in the best cases, where the child duplicates this or that idiosyncratic characteristic of the previous personality.

The last alternative theory Ian Stevenson considers at length is possession—the notion that the child is "possessed," taken over, controlled, by a discarnate personality.

He points out that in most of the credible cases of prima facie possession, the purported spirit remained in control for a more or less short period—the longest on record probably being the case of Lurrancy Vennum, in which the personality of the deceased Mary Roff controlled Lurrancy's body for some three months. However, in nearly all cases, the occupancy of the body by the possessing entity has been limited to a few days or a few weeks, or, if it is extended over a longer period, it is sporadically so.

In most of the reincarnation cases, the awareness of the previous personality is continuous for a period of at least several years.

Also, in possession cases, the primary personality is more or less displaced by the intruder. There is what Stevenson calls "a substitution of one personality for another." This does not happen in the typical reincarnation case. The primary personality remains intact and perceives itself as a continuation of the previous personality.

Stevenson allows that many of the cases he has investigated have weaknesses. In order to strengthen the evidence, he wants more cases that meet the following criteria:

The two families—that of the present and previous personality, respectively—have not met, thus ruling out the possibility of their having mingled memories.

There are several birthmarks involved, in different locations, and medical documentation is available for the marks on the previous personality.

The child demonstrates xenoglossy—the ability to speak fluently a language not learned.

As part of his continuing research, Ian Stevenson has launched a program in planned reincarnation. People are invited to register and describe the features they hope to produce in their next incarnation. The idea is that future investigators will then try to match these features with cases of apparent rebirth.

This is a copy of the registration form:

A.
Name . . . . Sex . . . .
Present Address . . . .
Date of Birth . . . . Place of
                            Birth . . . .
Date of   Age at

171

Registration . . . . Registration . . . .
Race . . . . Height . . . . Weight . . .
Color of Eyes . . . . . . Color of Hair . . .
Important Marks
on Skin, eg., Scars . . . .
Photograph   Age When
Taken At . . . . Photograph Taken . .
Tape Recording Made   Age When
for Voiceprint on . . . . Tape Recorded . . .
Photograph   Fingerprint

B. INFORMATION ABOUT PRESENT LIFE

1. Do you have any strong feelings about the circumstances, including family, into which you were born in this life? Mention finding the environment, or particular members of your family, specially pleasing or displeasing.

2. Have you had any particular physical deficiency or disease which seems of special importance to you? If so, please describe briefly.

3. Are you aware of any particular mental or behavioral trait which has been of special importance to you—negatively or positively? If so, please describe briefly.

4. Do you have a feeling of "unfinished business" about this life? This could be something you have worked on either externally, e.g., a book, or internally, e.g., a trait of character, which you want to finish later. If so, please describe briefly.

5. What events of your present life seem to you most memorable, most likely to be remembered long after others have been forgotten?

6. What details of your present personality would be most specific (or perhaps unique) with regard to identifying you and no one else? In other words, what is most specific about you, which, if remembered by you in another life, would identify you as being the person you are now, reincarnated, and no one else? If there is nothing about you which you consider absolutely specific, list a number of important traits which together might make a significant pattern. Please answer this section in your handwriting so we have a record of this on file.

7. Some persons have an intuition about how old they will be at death and the manner of their deaths. If you have such an impression, please describe it.

8. Have you any apparent memories of a previous life or lives, o rany strong predilections, e.g., for particular countries or periods, which might derive from previous lives; or has a sensitive (or medium) in whom you had confidence ever made statements about a previous life for you which seemed worthy of attention? If so, please describe these experiences.

C. PLANS FOR NEXT INCARNATION

1. Where in general would you like to be reborn? Specify a particular country, if you have a preference, and such features of the *physical* environment as urban, rural, near the sea, in the mountains, etc.

2. Under what circumstances (e.g., social, educational, vocational opportunities) would you like to be reborn?

3. Are there particular persons with whom you would like to be associated in your next life? a. As members of the same family? Specify whether mother, daughter, son, etc. b. As friends, acquaintances, colleagues?

4. What special traits, capacities, etc., would you like to develop in another incarnation?

5. Is there some affliction, disability, situation, which you particularly wish to avoid in another incarnation?

6. Do you wish to change sex in your next incarnation?

7. If so, please say why.

8. What length of intermission would you like to have between lives?

9. How would you like to be occupied during a period of survival after death (with or without later reincarnation)?

10. Notwithstanding your *desires* for another life, do you have an *expectation* that you will be reborn in a particular time, place and with particular sex, parents, circumstances, etc.? (This question

173

is to sample intuitions about a future life which
may run counter to desires or may not.)

A final section of the planned reincarnation form is to
be filled out after the death of the registrant, by someone
who knew him well. It asks for the following information:

1. Date of Death . . . . . . Age at Death . . .
2. Place of Death . . . .
3. Cause of Death . . . .
4. "Last Minute" Changes of Plans, Wishes, etc., of
   the Deceased . . . .
5. Notes of Persons who have expressed an interest
   in having the registrant reborn in their family.
6. Comments on Characteristics or Practices, e.g., meditation, which might have a bearing on the ability
   to remember a previous life.

Information about registering in this program for
planned reincarnation can be requested by writing to:

Dr. Ian Stevenson
Division of Parapsychology
Department of Psychiatry
University of Virginia School of Medicine
Charlottesville, Virginia 22901. U.S.A.
The issue of reincarnation—whether we do live not
one but many earthly lives on our pilgrimage toward
some sort of ultimate goal, whatever that may prove to
be—is a profound and complex one.
It is not a subject for easy answers—although, to be
sure, the world is full of people of quite undistinguished
mental or moral endowments who are certain that secrets hidden from the wise have been revealed to them.
I find such claims less than convincing.
I put greater confidence in the empirical method of
researchers like Ian Stevenson. Only by the painstaking
accumulation of data, namely, more hard cases, and the
careful, seasoned analysis and assessment of such cases,
are we likely to arrive—if ever—at an answer to the
age-old question: If a man die shall he live again?
A friend of mine, a psychiatrist, who is a long-time
student of parapsychology, does not think that Ian Stevenson's data prove reincarnation. His reason?

174

Not that he finds reincarnation too crazy to be true—just the opposite.

"The universe is so complex," says my friend, "that reincarnation, bizarre as it seems to some people, probably is too simple. It's not crazy enough to be true. The truth must start when reincarnation leaves off. . . ."

At any rate. Dr. Stevenson hopes that reincarnation data will provide a more fruitful avenue of inquiry than some others in the past into the question of the nature of human personality and whether it survives physical death.

As he sees it, the more traditional (in the West at least) attempt to establish survival after death by mediumistic communications may have reached a dead-end. Perhaps, he suggests, we should start at the other end of the process.

"In mediumistic communications," Stevenson said, "we have the problem of proving that someone clearly dead still lives.

"In evaluating apparent memories of former incarnations, the problem consists in judging whether someone clearly living once died.

"This may prove the easier task, and if pursued with sufficient zeal and success, may contribute decisively to the question of survival."

My own feeling is that, on the basis of the evidence in this book alone in favor of human survival after death, the hard-core skeptic is on the defensive. He must come up with an alternative explanation—if he can—which makes sense of the startling array of facts brought to light. It seems to me that these facts strongly indicate that there is something in man which transcends time and space.

Index

177

181